La Fontaine's Bawdy

A complete list of titles in the Lockert Library appears on page 275

La Fontaine's Bawdy

Of Libertines, Louts, and Lechers

TRANSLATIONS FROM
THE *CONTES ET
NOUVELLES EN VERS*

BY NORMAN R. SHAPIRO

ILLUSTRATED BY DAVID SCHORR

PRINCETON UNIVERSITY PRESS, PRINCETON, N. J.

Library of Congress Cataloging-in-Publication Data

La Fontaine, Jean de, 1621–1695.
[Contes et nouvelles en vers. English. Selections]
La Fontaine's bawdy : of libertines, louts,
and lechers : translations from the Contes et nouvelles
en vers / by Norman R. Shapiro.
p.   cm.—(Lockert library of poetry in translation)
Includes bibliographical references.
ISBN 0-691-06956-5 (CL)—ISBN 0-691-01532-5 (PA)
1. Bawdy poetry—France—Translations into English.
I. Shapiro, Norman R. II. Title. III. Series.
PQ1811.E4S5   1992
841'.4—dc20   92-2648

The Lockert Library of Poetry in Translation
is supported by a bequest from
Charles Lacy Lockert (1888–1974)

This book has been composed in Linotron Janson

Princeton University Press books are printed on
acid-free paper, and meet the guidelines for
permanence and durability of the Committee on Production
Guidelines for Book Longevity of the
Council on Library Resources

Printed in the United States of America

10 9 8 7 6 5 4 3 2 1

10 9 8 7 6 5 4 3 2 1
(Pbk.)

To the memory of four loving parents

Eva and Harry Shapiro
Iris and Hyman Schorr

Contents

CONTENTS

CONTENTS

Preface and Acknowledgments

In the spring of 1989 I was offered a commission to translate the voluminous correspondence of a famous modern French writer and his lover. To do so would have meant postponing a project that had been playing around in my head for some time: a translation from Jean de La Fontaine's *Contes et nouvelles en vers* to complement a collection I had done of his *Fables* a few years before. I would probably still be slogging through the reams of affectionate chitchat and socio-artistico-literary gossip if I had accepted. One thing is sure. I certainly would not have been able to spend the three months of the ensuing summer in the labor of love that produced the present volume.

The epistolary confessions of the poet-playwright-novelist and his friend might have proven more instructive and useful to the scholarly world of letters. (They might even, possibly, have proven more prurient in their own way than La Fontaine's spicy tales; but that's another matter.) For myself, however, they would not have given me nearly as much pleasure. Or maybe "fun" is a better word. I make no bones about my basic hedonism as a translator. Translation, for me, is both artistic re-creation and personal recreation. I have said it elsewhere but I think it bears repeating. That being the case, the choice of La Fontaine needs no explanation or excuse. He is an utter joy to work on, to work over, to work out; and—in an almost mystical relationship that transcends the passage of time—to work with. My apologies to the other author and his lover for the slight. (They're both dead now anyway so I don't think they'll care.) But first things first.

That decision made, the tales that I chose to translate—roughly half of La Fontaine's seventy-odd—offer a good cross-section of the variety of the corpus: the early, the later, the posthumous; the very long, the very short, the in-between; those written in the spate of then-standard line lengths as well as in the flexible La Fontaine *vers libres*; the straightforwardly narrative and the semidramatic; the frankly bawdy, the mildly suggestive, and even a few that wouldn't raise a vicar's eyebrow. (But not too many.) As for the translations, it should go without saying that I have tried not only to respect scrupulously the content of the originals but also to reproduce in general, insofar as one can do so from language to language, their form and tone as well: the supple and subtle rhythms with their free-flowing *enjambements* and seemingly capricious cadences; the rhymes—outer and inner: aligned, abreast, aslant; the archaisms, the wordplay, the wit, the nuance... All so many challenges that make the translator's craft the pleasure (and fun) that it is.

My thanks to a cohort of many staunch friends and colleagues: to Evelyn Singer Simha, who, with her unrelenting good sense and artistic judgment, seconded my decision and helpfully watched these translations take shape; to David Schorr for his elegant illustrations and valued support throughout; to Gay Manifold and her talented cast—John Barlow, Brick Conway, Peter Frenzel, Doris Hallie, and Evie Manieri—for breathing theatrical life into a number of these pieces; to Joan Jurale, of Wesleyan University's Olin Memorial Library; to Lillian Bulwa, Sylvia and Allan Kliman, Seymour O. Simches, and Caldwell Titcomb, always generous with their encouragement; and to Robert E. Brown, of Princeton University Press, and my copyeditor, Lauren Oppenheim.

As ever, I am indebted for much inspiration to my late parents, to whose memory this volume is lovingly dedicated.

Prologue

Few of the hundreds of thousands of French (and non-French) students who have, over the generations, memorized their share of La Fontaine with varying degrees of assiduity and affection have known or would even suspect that the poet of the inimitable though often imitated *Fables* was also the author of some three-score and ten *Contes et nouvelles en vers*.[1] Many of their teachers, no doubt, have known; but most would not likely let on. At least not in the tender years when their charges would be committing to memory the likes of "Maître Corbeau, sur un arbre perché..." and dozens of other miniscenarios of sometimes debatable didactic value to the young, for all their charm, wisdom, and wit. But write these tales he did—throughout most of his long life, in fact: before, during, and after the composition of the most celebrated of his fables—even though the then-scandalous exercise threatened not only to get him in trouble with the Church but also to stand in the way of his coveted election to the Académie Française, the latter still something of a fledgling organization scarcely a generation old and not given to liberality in its literary or moral stances.[2]

As suggested, even the *Fables* were not really children's fare unalloyed. Not most of them at any rate. And not simply for the frequent ambiguity of their morals—the victimization of the weak, the triumph of the strong and unscrupulous—or their physical violence, decried by Rousseau, Lamartine, and others, but rather for the sophisticated worldview and accumulated life experience required of the reader (especially in the later books) exposed to moral, philosophical, social, and even theological reflections quite beyond the ken of even the more precocious of juveniles. The *Contes*, on the other hand, were considered just plain obscene.

Contemporaries and successors alike were to take La Fontaine to task for them.[3] Even the poet himself, with a typically sly disingenuousness, would acknowledge his off-color inspiration in occasional introductions and other pronouncements, sounding a mea culpa or two and promising to mend his wayward ways in the future. Promises whose fulfillment, happily, he continued to postpone, until a grudging (pro forma?) near-deathbed recantation.[4] Today few of us would consider these largely traditional tales in the Chaucerian vein more than pleasantly titillating: explicit in spots, to be sure, but so sophisticated in their treatment that even at their earthiest and most frankly anatomical it would be absurd to accuse La Fontaine of trafficking in smut. Still, today too there are readers, I am sure, who will take a kind of sentimental umbrage at discovering the La Fontaine of their childhood to be also the author—or at least the rearranger and transmitter—of these often bawdy narratives however elegantly presented. And that, despite the fact that authentic pornography these days runs rampant and unabashed.

An anecdotal case in point. Last year a colleague of mine in our theater department learned about my translations and decided that they would lend themselves nicely to a costumed dramatic reading. I couldn't have agreed more. It is a truism that all verse was originally intended to be recited; and if the heady cerebrations of post-nineteenth-century poets have departed from the bardic, oral roots of their art, such was certainly not the case with seventeenth-century poets, especially those who wrote narrative verse with a distinctly dramatic flavor. And so, with my unstinting blessing, my colleague, Professor Gay Manifold, put together a selection of the present tales—including some of the more explicit, I might add—cleverly and artistically distributing the roles of narrator and assorted characters among a group of student actors and, for the more mature parts, a couple of faculty members. But when the actual texts were read at the first runthrough, one of our faculty colleagues, who had enthusiastically agreed to play a role, sight unseen, recoiled in utter disbelief and respectfully bowed out. Now, let me hasten to add that he is no bluenose. He had, however, been weaned on the *Fables* and, despite his sixty-plus years, seemed to feel almost betrayed by the disparity between his expectation of the "typical" La Fontaine, companion of his childhood innocence, and the reality of the texts themselves whose existence he had never suspected. How could La Fontaine, at this late date, sound such a discordant note in the harmonies of his youthful recollection! His reaction may, indeed, have been a little extreme; but I would be surprised if it weren't shared by a number of his generation, though few might want to admit it with such fidelity to principle at the risk of being twitted for prudery. (He was, by the way, replaced, and the performances were a huge success.) My intent here, of course, is not to establish some absolute "bawdy count" in the *Contes*—to condemn or defend—but merely to point out that for many a La Fontaine enthusiast, like our professor-cum-actor, any amount at all is a source of disillusion. On the other hand, I doubt that, were he an admirer of, say, Ronsard or Verlaine, he would be equally disenchanted to learn of those poets' sizable body of bawdy verse. Ronsard and Verlaine, after all, were never cradle-gurus or mentors of the growing-up years, recalled with nostalgia.

That said, it must be pointed out that the question of bawdiness is not the only ground on which the *Contes* and the *Fables* significantly differ. The most immediately striking dissimilarity, on even a casual observation, is in their lengths. While readers will find a few of the tales as short as—or shorter than—La Fontaine's average fable, in most of them he indulges his evident delight in leisurely narration, replete with detail, parenthesis, and authorial intervention at almost every turn of phrase. But even at their longest and densest the tales would, I think, bore only the most dyspeptic. And even if read from cover to cover, all of a piece (which, admittedly, is not the best way to approach them), they display enough variety of form to avoid monotony: traditional "four-square" alexandrines, decasyllables, and octosyllables reminiscent of Old French prosody; occasional narrative with dialogue interspersed; a full-fledged one-act comedy and an authentic *ballade* (neither translated here), and frequent recurring refrains of pseudoballadic flavor... And, of course, a dose of those wondrously pliable *vers libres* that were to be the hallmark of the *Fables*: that "formless" form of maximum freedom within restraint that La Fontaine handled with such dexterity and that almost all his fabulist-imitators were to copy, with varying degrees of success.[5] Curiously, he himself used the *vers libres* rather sparingly in the *Contes*—in less than a quarter of them—despite his opinion, voiced early in their composition while supposedly looking for the most appropriate vehicle for his rhymes, that "les vers irréguliers ayant un air qui tient beaucoup de la prose, cette manière pourroit sembler la plus naturelle, et par conséquent la meilleure" [being that lines of irregular length have rather an air of prose about them, that manner would seem the most natural and, therefore, the best].[6]

No less obvious than the difference in lengths is the difference in narrative personnel: flesh-and-blood human beings in the *Contes* as opposed to the usual humanoid animals (with occasional plants and even less frequent inanimate objects) of the *Fables*. But this basic distinction between the two genres had always been a little fuzzy around the edges, often honored more in the breach than in the observance, by La Fontaine himself as well as his predecessors, and would continue to be by his followers. Examples of human actors in the fable genre are not hard to come by in the canon, from the prototypical Aesop through the medieval *ysopets* and beyond. The reverse, however, would appear to be a rarity. If people sometimes people the fable—La Fontaine's and others'—animals, on the contrary, seldom if ever "people" the *conte*. As "props," perhaps; but as characters, hardly.

The reason, I think, can be found in another of the differences between the two genres; that is, the supposedly didactic aim of the fable in contrast to the gratuitously narrative raison d'être of the merely entertaining tale. I say "supposedly" because no one will ever convince me that La Fontaine really gave two raps for the moral content of his fables. Even in the first six books, written ostensibly for the edification of the Dauphin, and in the preface to which he pays lip service to the elevated ideal of guiding the young in the ways of righteousness, his *morales*, whether explicitly enunciated or left to be inferred, seem to take a back seat to rhetoric, style, wit, dramatic effect, and general artistic brio. I think that if we could somehow take La Fontaine aside in confidence we could get him to admit it, probably with a knowing wink. Now, once in a while one of his *Contes* will end with something of a moral. "On ne s'avise jamais de tout" [The Best-Laid Plans], here, is a good example. But it is clear—even clearer than in the *Fables*, where the form dictates that at least the fiction of didactic intent be preserved, through the traditional intermediary of animal heroes and villains—that the pleasure of telling a good (and racy) tale for its own sake far outweighs any possible useful lesson taught.

Contrasts in alleged didactic intent, in *dramatis personae* (or *dramatis animalia*, as the case may be), in length; bawdiness or non-bawdiness of subject—such differences between the *Fables* and the *Contes* are easily observable in comparing the works themselves. Not so another important difference of a more historico-literary nature. That is, the fact that while the ones spawned (and have continued to spawn) innumerable imitations, even to the present day, the others have had only a modest influence in comparison. French verse fabulists there were, to be sure, before La Fontaine. But it is, undeniably, his fables and not theirs that were the source—the watershed—of the flood that was to follow. Where, however, are the dozens of Furetières, Lamottes, Florians, Jauffrets, Arnaults, Anouilhs, and others of the *conte en vers*? The answer is that, while occasional literati over the years continued to versify tales in the lusty *esprit gaulois* tradition, no doubt in emulation—the name of the poet Grécourt, synonymous with licentiousness to the eighteenth century, comes to mind as a prime example—verse, which had been less and less holding its own against prose as a narrative vehicle since the Renaissance, was in gradual but inevitable retreat. Not even the prestige of a La Fontaine could rescue for long a basically anachronistic genre.[7] But if that prestige produced far fewer, and less impressive, *conteurs*-imitators than fabulist-imitators, it is not a denigration of his *Contes* to note that disparity. The comparison, rather, is a tribute to the long-lived vitality and generative power of the *Fables*. The latter unloosed a torrent; the former turned on a trickle.

Indeed, even while La Fontaine was practicing it the genre was something of a mild anachronism. One can rightly ask, then, why he elected to swim against the tide and use verse for his tales, especially when most of his important models, the likes of Boccaccio, Rabelais, the *Cent Nouvelles Nouvelles*, Marguerite de Navarre, Bonaventure Des Périers, and others—Ariosto was the most notable exception—had composed theirs in prose; and why, furthermore, he chose a verse that was, even in his own day, intentionally salted and peppered with archaisms of vocabulary, idiom, and style, quite unlike the *Fables*, still a-borning, as he himself confides: "D'autre part aussi le vieux langage, pour les choses de cette nature, a des grâces que celui de notre siècle n'a

pas" [Besides, the old language, for things of this type, has beau-
ties that the language of our own time has not].[8] Whatever other
literary explanations might be brought to bear, the basic reply to
the first of these questions has to be self-evident. La Fontaine was
a poet to the tips of his fingers. It is rather like asking why the
great Victor Hugo, through whatever casuistic twists of logic,
could obstinately write his romantic dramas in verse when, at the
same time, he was militating in his celebrated preface to *Cromwell*
against the arbitrary and unrealistic separation of the tragic and
comic genres, and other conventional artificialities of the classical
theater. One doesn't, after all, ask a bee why it makes honey. So
too with La Fontaine. As for the question of intentional archa-
ism, he answers it himself in the passage just cited. His *Contes*
are a conscious stylistic look backward: a literary link not only
with his more recent story-telling predecessors—Rabelais, Mar-
guerite, and such—but also with the even more remote *fabliaux*
of the medieval tradition.

But if the *Contes* represent such a link with his narrative past,
they are no less firmly rooted in the "authorial present": that po-
tential immediacy any author establishes with every potential au-
dience. And, in La Fontaine's case, an "authorial present" all the
more reinforced by his pervasive "authorial presence." By this I
mean that, more than most poets, narrative ones especially, he is
always keenly aware of his readers (or, ideally, his listeners) out
there in the Great Literary Beyond, waiting to make eventual
contact with them. And they, conversely, with him; easily, since
few authors, I think, establish as direct a rapport with their au-
dience—a "complicity," as I like to describe it. No less in the
Contes than in the prototypical *Fables*. In this respect, despite the
several differences suggested, both collections share in the de-
lights of La Fontaine's very intimate style, abetted by that tech-
nical mastery of rhyme and rhythm that makes it all flow so ef-
fortlessly, and look and sound so easy: the same unhurried pace,
dictated—if I may borrow an unexpected comparison, like a
game of baseball, as poet Donald Hall describes it—by its own
inner imperatives; the same delectation in digression; the same
offhand commentary whenever the spirit moves him to it... In
short, the author's constant presence at the reader's elbow, each
time bringing to life a work that links him—as well as to his

past—to the eternal present of every new or repeated reading, every confrontation with the text irrespective of time or space.

It is certainly for such poetic and narrative talents that La Fontaine's "libertines, louts, and lechers" attract and engage us—and through them, of course, La Fontaine himself—and not for the frequent bawdiness of their escapades, tricks, triumphs, and tribulations. Now, whatever attracts exerts power, and one needn't be a disciple of Foucault (or even understand him) to appreciate the notion that the play of power is fundamental to literary works, and to narrative more than most. The author of any narrative is engaged, ipso facto, in a twofold power relationship with the reader. First, simply—or simplistically—because as narrator, by definition, he or she always knows something that the reader does not, and that knowledge confers power; and, second, because in narrating it to the reader the author undertakes to oblige the latter to continue the encounter: in other words, to keep reading. La Fontaine's celebrated duo of the crow and the fox—Maîtres Corbeau and Renard, of near-universal fame (*Fables* 1.2)—can be taken, not too exaggeratedly I think, as paradigmatic of this author-reader relationship. Our narrator-Fox delivers his "text" to the enthralled receptor-Crow, who, as long as he keeps listening, tacitly acknowledges the power of the "author" poised there beneath him. (Indeed, a paradoxical positioning given the latter's implied superiority, but one obviously necessitated—gravity being what it is—by his ultimate goal: Maître Corbeau's hunk of cheese.) But this play of power between them is ambivalent; until, that is, the dénouement of Fox's textual recitation. Crow, after all, could just as easily fly away—that is, stop listening and terminate the encounter—and thereby quite simply reverse the power dynamic. (My more perceptive students often ask me why he doesn't.) So too a reader can always stop reading and close the book. But clearly the attraction of Fox's "text" is too powerful for Crow, and Fox comes out on top. (Dynamically if not spatially.) Likewise any author who keeps the reader reading to the end.

In the case of the encounters between readers of the *Contes* and La Fontaine, as well as with the better-known and more approachable *Fables*, few, I venture, would be tempted to exert their potential "reader power," as it were. All of which is only a high-flown way of expressing an old cliché in properly theoretical terminology: to wit, "It's hard to put a good book down." At least so I have found it in my own confrontation with the gently persuasive power of La Fontaine's narrative art. Perhaps through these translations others either unfamiliar with the original French or uncomfortable with its intentional archaism will find it so too. I hope so. Literature, after all, is one power game in which the "loser," acknowledging the author's mastery and his own subordination to it, always ultimately comes out the winner.

Bibliographical Note

The bibliography of books, monographs, articles, and notes on La Fontaine is staggering to say the least, and constantly growing. Biographies of the poet and studies of his *Fables*, general and specialized, abound in French, English, and most other Western languages; and their titles are too readily available to researchers to need repetition here. The *Contes et nouvelles en vers*, on the other hand, have been much less extensively or intensively treated.

Of the several modern editions the most useful for scholarly purposes remains Henri Regnier's monumental eleven-volume *Œuvres complètes de Jean de la Fontaine* in the series Les Grands Écrivains de la France (Paris: Hachette, 1883–92), of which volumes 4, 5 and 6 are devoted to the *Contes*. Regnier's exhaustive and often exhausting notes, almost to the point of overkill, give the provenance of the individual tales where known—thus supplementing La Fontaine's own occasional explicit or implicit indications—as well as a mine of other literary and linguistic detail. Of easier access to present-day readers are the following less venerable editions of the *Contes et nouvelles en vers*, arranged here by date, most of which also contain a variety of more modest introductions, chronologies, appendices, and notes:

Clarac, Pierre, ed. 2 vols. Paris: Société les Belles Lettres, 1934.

Groos, René, and Jacques Schiffrin, eds. In *Fables, contes et nouvelles*. Bibliothèque de la Pléiade. Paris: Gallimard, 1954.

Zeugschmitt, Jacqueline, ed. 2 vols. Collection Nationale des Grands Auteurs. Paris: Imprimerie Nationale, 1959–60.

Couton, Georges, ed. Paris: Gallimard, 1961.

Ferrier, Nicole, and Jean-Pierre Collinet, eds. Paris: Garnier-Flammarion, 1980.

Bassy, Alain-Marie, ed. Collection Folio. Paris: Gallimard, 1982.

Bibliothèque Lattès. Paris: Éditions Jean-Claude Lattès, 1990.

The text I have used is from the Clarac edition of 1934, reproduced with all its archaisms and vagaries of spelling and punctuation, except for a few obvious misprints.

Studies of the *Contes* are, surprisingly, rather sparse. Of interest, more to academics than to lay readers, are the following:

Cauley, Joseph C. "The *Contes* of La Fontaine: A Study in Narrative Mode." Ph.D. dissertation, University of Wisconsin, 1972.

————. "Narrative Techniques in the *Contes et nouvelles en vers* of La Fontaine." In *The French Short Story*. University of South Carolina French Literature Series, no. 2 (1975): 27–38.

Collinet, Jean-Pierre. "La Matière et l'art du prologue dans les *Contes* de La Fontaine." In *Studi francesi* (May–August 1981): 219–37.

Genot, Gérard. "La Fontaine et Bocace." In *Il Boccaccio nella cultura francese*, ed. Carlo Pellegrini, pp. 567–79. Florence: Olschki, 1971.

————. "Le Récit du déclassé, Boccace et La Fontaine." In *Revue romane* 7 (1972): 204–32.

Grisé, Catherine. "Le Jeu de l'imitation: un Aspect de la réception des *Contes* de La Fontaine." In *Papers on French Seventeenth Century Literature* 10, no. 18 (1983): 249–62.

Grisé, Catherine, and Jean Varloot, eds. "Les *Contes* de La Fontaine: Préhistoire d'un genre." In *Du Baroque aux Lumières*. Limoges: Rougerie, 1986.

Howard, Fannie Scott. "Illusion and Reality in the *Contes* of La Fontaine." *Dissertation Abstracts* 31 (1970–71): 2919 A.

————. "La Fontaine on Fiction Writing: Reality and Illusion in the *Contes*." In *The French Short Story*. University of South Carolina French Literature Series, no. 2 (1975): 167–72.

La Fontaine, Gilles E. de. "Les *Contes* de La Fontaine et les contemporains." In *Présence francophone* 3 (1971): 94–102.

————. *La Fontaine dans ses "Contes": Profil de l'homme d'après ses confidences*. Sherbrooke: Éditions Naaman, 1978.

Lapp, John Clarke. *The Esthetics of Negligence: La Fontaine's "Contes."* Cambridge: Cambridge University Press, 1971.

Merino-Morais, Jane. *Différence et répétition dans les "Contes" de La Fontaine*. Gainesville: University Presses of Florida, 1983.

Soriano, Marc. "Des *Contes* aux *Fables*." In *Europe* 515 (March 1972): 99–131.

Timm, Joachim. "Erzähltechnik bei La Fontaine und Boccaccio. Ein Vergleich der *Contes* und ihrer Vorlagen in *Decameron*." Ph.D. dissertation, University of Hamburg, 1963.

La Fontaine's Bawdy

Le Cocu, battu, et content

Nouvelle tirée de Bocace

N'a pas long-temps de Rome revenoit
Certain Cadet qui n'y profita guere;
Et volontiers en chemin sejournoit,
Quand par hazard le Galand rencontroit
Bon vin, bon giste, et belle chambriere.
Avint qu'un jour en un Bourg arresté
Il vid passer une Dame jolie,
Leste, pimpante, et d'un Page suivie,
Et la voyant il en fut enchanté.
La convoita; comme bien sçavoit faire.
Prou de pardons il avoit rapporté;
De vertu peu; chose assez ordinaire.
La Dame estoit de gracieux maintien,
De doux regard, jeune, fringante et belle;
Somme qu'enfin il ne luy manquoit rien,
Fors que d'avoir un Amy digne d'elle.
Tant se la mit le drosle en la cervelle,
Que dans sa peau peu ny point ne duroit:
Et s'informant comment on l'appelloit:
C'est, luy dit-on, la Dame du Village.
Messire Bon l'a prise en mariage,
Quoy qu'il n'ait plus que quatre cheveux gris:
Mais comme il est des premiers du païs,
Son bien supplée au défaut de son âge.
Nostre Cadet tout ce détail apprit,
Dont il conceut esperance certaine.
Voicy comment le Pelerin s'y prit.
Il renvoya dans la Ville prochaine
Tous ses Valets; puis s'en fut au chasteau:

The Cuckold, Cudgeled but Contented

A certain young *abbé*—blithe, devil-may-care—
Was wending home from Rome.[1] His sojourn there
Had profited him little. For whenever
He found good wine, good bed (and good, as well—
To fill said bed—some goodly *demoiselle*),
He would have lived the traveler's life forever.
It came to pass one day that, passing by,
Attended by her page (and passing fair),
A lady—comely, pert, young, debonair:
In short, a perfect beauty—caught his eye.
No sooner spied than lusted after, she!
And he? Well versed in guile, I guarantee,
But bringing precious little virtue back
From Rome, as you might guess; though full his pack
With papal dispensations, cap-a-pie.
Well then, what does the cleric bold discover?
That nothing has milady to desire—
Nothing, that is, save for a worthy lover!
Yearning to play the part, our ardent sire,
Tingling—nay, burning!—with love's passion-fire,
Inquires who she may be; learning thereat
That Messire Bon, the town's aristocrat,
Is wedded to Madame: a country squire—
Old, bald, but rich. (What better consolation!)
The pilgrim, thus apprised, quickly conceived
Much hope for sweet success; for he believed
Sure victory would crown his expectation.
Indeed, not for a moment did he doubt it.
As for his plan, here's how he goes about it.
He sends his servants on ahead, whilst he

Dit qu'il estoit un jeune Jouvenceau,
Qui cherchoit maistre, et qui sçavoit tout faire.
Messire Bon fort content de l'affaire
Pour Fauconnier le loüa bien et beau.
(Non toutesfois sans l'avis de sa femme)
Le Fauconnier plût tres-fort à la Dame;
Et n'estant homme en tel pourchas nouveau,
Guere ne mit à declarer sa flâme.
Ce fut beaucoup; car le Vieillard estoit
Fou de sa femme, et fort peu la quittoit,
Sinon les jours qu'il alloit à la chasse.
Son Fauconnier, qui pour lors le suivoit,
Eust demeuré volontiers en sa place.
La jeune Dame en estoit bien d'accord,
Ils n'attendoient que le temps de mieux faire.
Quand je diray qu'il leur en tardoit fort,
Nul n'osera soustenir le contraire.
Amour enfin, qui prit à cœur l'affaire,
Leur inspira la ruse que voicy.
La Dame dit un soir à son mary:
Qui croyez-vous le plus remply de zele
De tous vos gens? Ce propos entendu
Messire Bon luy dit: J'ay toûjours creu
Le Fauconnier garçon sage et fidelle;
Et c'est à luy que plus je me fierois.
—Vous auriez tort, repartit cette Belle;
C'est un méchant: il me tint l'autrefois
Propos d'amour, dont je fus si surprise,
Que je pensay tomber tout de mon haut;
Car qui croiroit une telle entreprise?
Dedans l'esprit il me vint aussi-tost

Presents himself *chez* Messire Bon, the spouse,
Stating, with show of youthful *bonhomie*
(And much pretense!), that he, in truth, would be
Honored to serve the master of the house.
His Excellence consents, and with great joy—
Nor, by the by, without his wife's opinion—
Welcomes the young *abbé* to his employ,
To be his falconer. The would-be minion,
Finding much pleasure in the lady's eyes—
Not new to such endeavor!—promptly plies
The belle with surreptitious declaration.
And clever, he, to find a way. Time and again
He tries. But such the husband's adulation,
That never does he leave her side; save when
He goes off on the hunt, perforce. And then,
Much though the gallant would have stayed behind,
The husband would have been suspicious, surely.
Yet find a way he does. And she, demurely,
Makes clear that she reciprocates in kind.
The question now remains: how, when, and where
Might they do more than talk? How might the pair
Find circumstance auspicious to their passion?
Taking their plight to heart, Love, in his fashion,
Inspired them with a ruse. Here's what they did.
One day, the wife, in conversation, bid
Her husband tell which of his retinue
He found to be, of all, the faithfulest.
To which Messire, replying, said he guessed
That, giving each and every one his due,
Yet was his falconer the one he must
Deem without doubt the worthiest of his trust.
"Heaven forfend! What a misapprehension!"

De l'étrangler, de luy manger la veuë:
Il tint à peu; je n'en fus retenuë,
Que pour n'oser un tel cas publier:
Mesme, à dessein qu'il ne le pûst nier,
Je fis semblant d'y vouloir condescendre;
Et cette nuit sous un certain poirier
Dans le jardin je luy dis de m'attendre.
Mon mary, dis-je, est toûjours avec moy,
Plus par amour que doutant de ma foy;
Je ne me puis dépestrer de cet homme,
Sinon la nuit pendant son premier somme:
D'auprés de luy taschant de me lever,
Dans le jardin je vous iray trouver.
Voila l'estat où j'ay laissé l'affaire.
Messire Bon se mit fort en colere.
Sa femme dit: Mon mary, mon Epoux,
Jusqu'à tantost cachez vostre courroux;
Dans le jardin attrapez-le vous mesme;
Vous le pourrez trouver fort aisément;
Le poirier est à main gauche en entrant.
Mais il vous faut user de stratagême:
Prenez ma juppe, et contre-faites-vous;
Vous entendrez son insolence extrême:
Lors d'un baston donnez-luy tant de coups,
Que le Galant demeure sur la place.
Je suis d'avis que le friponneau fasse
Tel compliment à des femmes d'honneur!
L'Espoux retint cette leçon par cœur.
Onc il ne fut une plus forte dupe
Que ce vieillard, bon-homme au demeurant.
Le temps venu d'attraper le Galant,

Answers the wife. "Why, just the other day
That wretch approached me in most shameless way
And spoke of love in words I dare not mention.
Shocked as I was, I sighed: 'Ah me! Oh my!'
And had a mind to strangle him, believe me,
There on the spot. But then, 'Nay, nay,' thought I,
'People will talk. Besides, he would deny
His villainy, unless I much deceive me.
Rather,' I mused, 'I'll feign that I agree.'
So to the garden shall he come this night,
Under a pear tree, there to wait for me.
'My husband never leaves me from his sight,'
I told him. 'Not for lack of trust, I vow,
But for excess of love...' Well, anyhow,
Then I explained the only time I might
Be rid of you, monsieur, is when you're sleeping.
Thus will your 'faithful' falconer be keeping
Tonight (or so he thinks!) his shameful tryst."
Sire flies into a rage. Wife cautions: "Hist!
Best save your ire, my love. Better you vent it
Yourself upon our foul noctambulist,
Caught in his crime. Best you make him repent it!
No trouble shall you have to catch him there.
The tree is by the garden-gate: a pear,
Off on the left. And yet, still must you use
Some wile, some proper stratagem... Here, wear
My skirt. Disguise yourself like me. The ruse
Will show you how the faithless blackguard—dash him!—
Would thus abuse your trust. Then shall you thrash him,
Throttle him, thresh him, smash him—head to limb—
And teach him that I want no part of him,
Like any honest lady!" Hearing this,

Messire Bon se couvrit d'une juppe,
S'encorneta, courut incontinent
Dans le jardin, où ne trouva personne:
Garde n'avoit: car tandis qu'il frissonne,
Claque des dents, et meurt quasi de froid,
Le Pelerin, qui le tout observoit,
Va voir la Dame; avec elle se donne
Tout le bon-temps qu'on a, comme je croy,
Lors qu'amour seul estant de la partie
Entre deux draps on tient femme jolie;
Femme jolie, et qui n'est point à soy.
Quand le Galant un assez bon espace
Avec la Dame eust esté dans ce lieu,
Force luy fut d'abandonner la place:
Ce ne fut pas sans le vin de l'adieu.
Dans le jardin il court en diligence.
Messire Bon remply d'impatience
A tous momens sa paresse maudit.
Le Pelerin, d'aussi loin qu'il le vid,
Feignit de croire appercevoir la Dame,
Et luy cria: Quoy donc méchante femme!
A ton mary tu brassois un tel tour!
Est-ce le fruit de son parfait amour!
Dieu soit témoin que pour toy j'en ay honte:
Et de venir ne tenois quasi conte,
Ne te croyant le cœur si perverti,
Que de vouloir tromper un tel mary.
Or bien, je vois qu'il te faut un amy;
Trouvé ne l'as en moy, je t'en asseure.
Si j'ay tiré ce rendez-vous de toy,
C'est seulement pour éprouver ta foy:

Messire considers what she says, thinks on it,
Rehearses, step by step, the artifice…
Come night, then will he take the skirt and don it,
Make for the garden, where—poor, arrant gull!—
He shivers in his bonnet, teeth a-chatter.
What does he find there? No one: nought, nil, null!
Meanwhile, all eyes and ears, our pilgrim-satyr
Visits the old fool's wife; and with the latter
Dallies and toys to heart's content, there doing
All of those boudoir deeds—with, to, and at her—
That wanton Love demands. In hours ensuing,
When all is said and done, and time is up,
He leaves (but not without the stirrup-cup!),
Runs to the tree, where, cursing his delay,
Messire still waits. The falconer-*abbé*
No sooner catches sight of his curmudgeon
Than, shamming great dismay, in highest dudgeon,
He feigns to think that it's the wife he sees:
"O shameless hussy! Brazen jade! So! Would
You thus dishonor such a spouse? So good,
So kind, so loving? Fie! What ways are these?
Oh, the disgrace of your iniquities!
God knows, I almost failed to come. How could
A wife like his defile her womanhood?
How could I think that you had acquiesced?
You want a lover? Aye! That's plain to see,
Vile baggage! Well, you'll not find one in me!
I called you here, madame, merely to test
The strength of your supposed fidelity;
Not to be lured by you into a life
Of lechery and sin! O wicked wife!

Et ne t'attends de m'induire à luxure:
Grand pecheur suis; mais j'ay, la Dieu mercy,
De ton honneur encor quelque soucy.
A Monseigneur ferois-je un tel outrage?
Pour toy, tu viens avec un front de Page:
Mais, foy de Dieu, ce bras te chastiera;
Et Monseigneur puis aprés le sçaura.
Pendant ces mots l'Epoux pleuroit de joye,
Et tout ravy disoit entre ses dents:
Loüé soit Dieu, dont la bonté m'envoye
Femme et Valet si chastes, si prudens.
Ce ne fut tout; car à grands coups de gaule
Le Pelerin vous lui froisse une épaule;
De horions laidement l'accoustra;
Jusqu'au logis ainsi le convoya.
Messire Bon eust voulu que le zele
De son valet n'eust esté jusques-là;
Mais le voyant si sage et si fidelle,
Le bon-hommeau des coups se consola.
Dedans le lit sa femme il retrouva;
Luy conta tout, en luy disant: Mamie,
Quand nous pourrions vivre cent ans encor,
Ny vous ny moy n'aurions de nostre vie
Un tel valet; c'est sans doute un tresor.
Dans nostre Bourg je veux qu'il prenne femme:
A l'avenir traitez-le ainsi que moy.
—Pas n'y faudray, luy repartit la Dame;
Et de cecy je vous donne ma foy.

A sinner like the rest I surely am;
Still is your virtue my concern, madame,
By God! Why, can you think I would betray
Messire, my lord? Nay, nay! I could not do it.
Here come you, wench, with insolent display,
To do your will—your ill! Well shall you rue it!
Now will this arm chastise your fell offense,
And shall your husband learn the truth!" Throughout
The lying scoundrel's virtuous eloquence
Messire weeps tears of joy, and burbles out
Muted hosannas to both spouse and servant—
Creatures so good, devoted, prudent, chaste...
Affecting rage—the lout!—and outrage fervent,
Monsieur proceeds to pummel, batter, baste
Messire's poor back, and sends him home—a-welt,
A-wound—delighted at his minion's zeal
(Though wishing it might be less sorely felt!);
For glad is he to pardon blows thus dealt,
Seeing the wealth of homage they reveal.
He finds his wife abed; shows her his deal
Of blacks-and-blues, each bruise; then tells her why,
Praising his young retainer to the sky:
"Milady, we could seek since time began:
Never could you or I find such a man!
A woman must I get him; one close by.
My brother, he. Pray treat him, love, like me."
Says she: "Indeed..." (not too reluctantly);
"I shall, *messire*... At least, I'll surely try."

The Cuckold, Cudgeled but Contented

Le Mary confesseur

Conte tiré des Cent Nouvelles Nouvelles

Messire Artus sous le grand Roy François
Alla servir aux guerres d'Italie;
Tant qu'il se vid, aprés maints beaux exploits,
Fait Chevalier en grand'ceremonie.
Son General luy chaussa l'éperon:
Dont il croyoit que le plus haut Baron
Ne luy deust plus contester le passage.
Si s'en revient tout fier en son Village,
Où ne surprit sa femme en Oraison.
Seule il l'avoit laissée à la maison;
Il la retrouve en bonne compagnie,
Dansant, sautant, menant joyeuse vie,
Et des Muguets avec elle à foison.
Messire Artus ne prit goust à l'affaire;
Et ruminant sur ce qu'il devoit faire:
Depuis que j'ay mon Village quitté,
Si j'estois crû, dit-il, en dignité
De cocüage et de chevalerie:
C'est moitié trop, sçachons la verité.
Pour ce s'avise, un jour de Confrairie,
De se vestir en Prestre, et Confesser.
Sa femme vient à ses pieds se placer.
De prime abord sont par la bonne Dame
Expediez tous les pechez menus;
Puis à leur tour les gros estant venus,
Force luy fut qu'elle changeast de game.
Pere, dit-elle, en mon lit sont receus
Un Gentil-homme, un Chevalier, un Prêtre.
Si le Mary ne se fust fait connoistre,

The Husband Who Played Confessor

Back in the days of King François *premier*,
Messire Artus fought with such gallantry
And grit, in the Italian Wars, that he
Was made a proper knight: a *chevalier*.
His general, with solemn pomp, bestowed
The spurs; and promptly off our hero rode,
Back to his village, where (proud popinjay,
Deeming himself no less endowed, indeed—
Though newly dubbed—than duly pedigreed
Knight of the realm) he found his wife. In prayer?
As he had left her, unaccompanied?
No, not one whit. Rather, surrounded there
By beau and coxcomb, merrily disporting
With song and dance, and, in a word, cavorting.
Artus was less than pleased, to say the least.
Considering how best to rectify
Matters, he mused: "While at the wars, have I,
In knighthood and in dignity increased.
But if I've grown, as well, in cuckoldry,
Then too much have I grown, assuredly!
Now must I learn the truth." No doubt inspired
By crowds of pilgrims piously attired
To fete their saint, he has a mind to don
The priestly garb and go to hear confessions.
His wife arrives (this had he counted on),
Kneels at his feet, and—looking not upon
His face—reveals at first her indiscretions:
Modest, withal, these sins. But soon, instead,
Changing her tune, baring her gross transgressions:

Elle en alloit enfiler beaucoup plus;
Courte n'estoit pour seur la Kyrielle.
Son Mary donc l'interrompt là-dessus;
Dont bien luy prit. Ah, dit-il, infidelle!
Un Prestre mesme! à qui crois-tu parler?
—A mon mary, dit la fausse femelle,
Qui d'un tel pas se sceut bien démesler.
Je vous ay veu dans ce lieu vous couler,
Ce qui m'a fait douter du badinage.
C'est un grand cas qu'estant homme si sage,
Vous n'ayez sceu l'énigme débroüiller.
On vous a fait, dites-vous, Chevalier:
Auparavant vous estiez Gentil-homme:
Vous estes Prestre avecque ces habits.
—Benist soit Dieu, dit alors le bon-homme:
Je suis un sot de l'avoir si mal pris.

"*Mon père*," says she, "I've taken to my bed
A nobleman, a knight, a priest..." The litany
Would surely have continued had not he
Cut short the list. "Ah, wench! A priest as well?
Whom do you think you're telling, infidel?"
She, seeing through his sham and masquerade—
Clever and quick of wit, the shameless jade!—
Replies: "Why you, my husband, truth to tell.
For when I saw you lurking hereabout
I knew you must be bent on badinage.
Shrewd as you are, can you not figure out
The sense behind my pleasant persiflage?
Nobleman were you born; now knighted too;
And here, a priest! All three, *messire*, are you!"
"Blessed be the Lord!" the husband sighs, relieved.
"Ah, what a fool was I to be deceived."

Conte d'une chose arrivée à Chasteau-Thierry

Un Savetier, que nous nommerons Blaise,
Prit belle femme; et fut tres-avisé.
Les bonnes gens qui n'estoient à leur aise,
S'en vont prier un Marchand peu rusé,
Qu'il leur prêtast dessous bonne promesse
My-muid de grain; ce que le Marchand fait.
Le terme écheu, ce creancier les presse.
Dieu sçait pourquoy: le galant, en effet,
Crut que par là baiseroit la commere.
Vous avez trop dequoy me satisfaire,
(Ce luy dit-il) et sans débourser rien:
Accordez-moy ce que voux sçavez bien.
—Je songeray, répond-elle, à la chose.
Puis vient trouver Blaise tout aussi-tost,
L'avertissant de ce qu'on luy propose.
Blaise luy dit: Par bieu, femme, il nous faut
Sans coup ferir rattraper nostre somme.
Tout de ce pas allez dire à cet homme
Qu'il peut venir, et que je n'y suis point.
Je veux icy me cacher tout à point.
Avant le coup demandez la cedule.
De la donner je ne crois qu'il recule.
Puis tousserez afin de m'avertir;
Mais haut et clair, et plûtost deux fois qu'une.
Lors de mon coin vous me verrez sortir
Incontinent, de crainte de fortune.
Ainsi fut dit, ainsi s'executa.
Dont le mary puis aprés se vanta;
Si que chacun glosoit sur ce mystere.

Tale of an Event at Château-Thierry

A cobbler once there was—Blaise, let us call him—
Who took himself a wife of winsome air.
Wily was he, but poor. One day the pair
Went to the market, where, with promise solemn,
They begged a loan of grain. The merchant—one
Not practiced yet in ways of wile—relenting,
Lent them a load.[1] And yet, no simpleton
Was he. For when the debt fell due, presenting
Himself at their abode, he warns: "Time's up!"
Thinking, by God, that thereby might he tup
The fair *commère*, forced, thus, into consenting.
"More than enough have you to satisfy me"—
So he declares—"and you'll pay not one sou!
Grant me but what you know I want of you,
And shall your debt thereat be canceled by me."
"I'll think about it," she replies; then hies her
Therewith to husband Blaise, quick to advise her
Wherewith to beat the blackguard at his game.
Says he to her: "Zounds, woman! In the name…!
Go see the rogue. None will he be the wiser:
Tell him I'm gone… That he should come this night.
I'll hide. And you, before he tries to do you,
See that he gives our bill directly to you.
He'll not delay, if I judge him aright.
Now, lest he do the deed—you hear?—you cough.
And better twice than once… And loud, and clear!…
I'll come posthaste—no dawdling, have no fear!—
And straightway send the scoundrel running off."
No sooner said than done. Whereat our Blaise

Mieux eust valu tousser aprés l'affaire,
(Dit à la Belle un des plus gros Bourgeois)
Vous eussiez eu vostre conte tous trois.
N'y manquez plus, sauf aprés de se taire.
Mais qu'en est-il? or ça, Belle, entre nous.
Elle répond: Ah Monsieur! croyez-vous,
Que nous ayons tant d'esprit que vos Dames?
(Notez qu'illec avec deux autres femmes
Du gros Bourgeois l'épouse estoit aussi)
Je pense bien, continua la Belle,
Qu'en pareil cas Madame en use ainsi;
Mais quoy, chacun n'est pas si sage qu'elle.

Boasted about the trick for days and days.
Many's the tongue that wagged in idle chatter
Over his feat. One rich bourgeois observed:
"Madame, if you had coughed *after* the matter,
All three of you, I daresay, would be served.
Next time, if I were you..." She, in reply:
"Ah, sire, can you believe that such as I
Am shrewd as these beldames of high degree?
(His wife was, with two others, standing by.)
"I have no doubt, I vow, that, verily,
That's what madame, your wife, would do, monsieur.
But then, who can be clever, sire, like her!"

Conte tiré d'Athenée

Axiocus avec Alcibiades
Jeunes, bien-faits, galants, et vigoureux
Par bon accord comme grands camarades,
En mesme nid furent pondre tous deux.
Qu'arrive-il? l'un de ces amoureux
Tant bien exploite autour de la Donzelle,
Qu'il en nâquit une fille si belle,
Qu'ils s'en vantoient tous deux également.
Le temps venu que cet objet charmant
Pût pratiquer les leçons de sa mere;
Chacun des deux en voulut estre amant;
Plus n'en voulut, l'un ny l'autre estre pere.
Frere, dit l'un, ah! vous ne sçauriez faire
Que cet enfant ne soit vous tout craché.
—Parbieu, dit l'autre, il est à vous compere:
Je prends sur moy le hazard du peché.

Tale from Athenaeus

Axiochus and Alcibiades—
Two well-endowed and handsome gallants—go
Off to the selfsame furrow, there to sow
The wildest of their oats.[1] Now, one of these
Young lovers sows his seed, indeed, so well
That, as you might expect, the *demoiselle*
Brings forth a daughter; one, in fact, so fair
That each claims credit for the bagatelle.
In time the lass, lovely beyond compare,
Has learned her mother's lessons; such that, now,
Grown lustful of the belle, each of our pair,
No longer fatherly, will disavow
His claim. Says one: "But how can you deny
Your spit and image? Clearly she's your kin!"
"No! Yours!" the other parries in reply.
"Besides, for such a one I'll risk the sin."

Tale from Athenaeus

Autre conte tiré d'Athenée

A son souper un glouton,
Commande que l'on appreste
Pour luy seul un Esturgeon,
Sans en laisser que la teste.
Il soupe; il creve; on y court:
On luy donne maints clisteres.
On luy dit, pour faire court,
Qu'il mette ordre à ses affaires.
Mes amis, dit le goulu,
M'y voila tout resolu;
Et puis qu'il faut que je meure,
Sans faire tant de façon,
Qu'on m'apporte tout à l'heure
Le reste de mon poisson.

Another Tale from Athenaeus

A glutton, for his supper, bid
That he be brought a fish to eat:
A sturgeon, all for him, complete,
Save for the head. Bring it they did.
He sups... He bursts... As he lies dying,
To see what good they yet might do him
They hasten to his side, applying
Many an enema unto him,
Telling him his affairs ought be
Forthwith put right. "My friends," says he,
"Quite so. Now, since I'll soon be dead,
If you would grant my dying wish,
Please go and fetch that sturgeon-head:
I'd like to finish up my fish."

Another Tale from Athenaeus

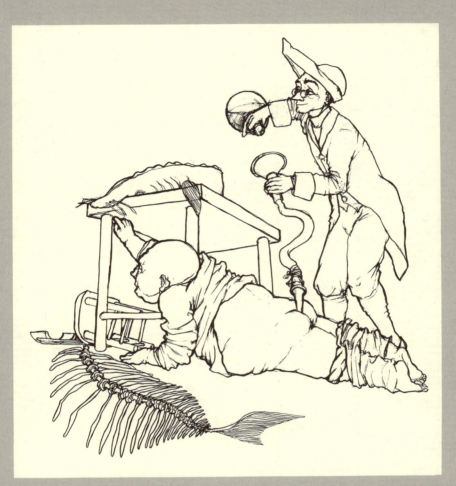

Conte de ****

Sœur Jeanne, ayant fait un poupon,
Jeûnoit, vivoit en sainte fille,
Toûjours estoit en oraison.
Et toûjours ses Sœurs à la grille.
Un jour donc l'Abbesse leur dit:
Vivez comme Sœur Jeanne vit;
Fuyez le monde et sa sequelle.
Toutes reprirent à l'instant:
Nous serons aussi sages qu'elle,
Quand nous en aurons fait autant.

Tale from ****

Having brought forth a chubby tot,
Good Sister Jeanne, in penitence,
Spends day and night in abstinence
And prayer—what saintly miss would not?—
While off a-prattling by the fence
Her sister nuns raise quite a stir.
The abbess chides: "See Sister Jeanne?
You should renounce the world, like her!"
And their reply: "We shall, each one,
After we've done what she has done."

Conte du juge de Mesle

Deux Avocats qui ne s'accordoient point,
Rendoient perplex un Juge de Province.
Si ne pût onc découvrir le vray point;
Tant luy sembloit que fust obscur et mince.
Deux pailles prend d'inégale grandeur:
Du doigt les serre; il avoit bonne pince.
La longue échet sans faute au deffendeur,
Dont renvoyé s'en va gay comme un Prince.
La Cour s'en plaint, et le Juge repart:
Ne me blâmez, Messieurs, pour cet égard:
De nouveauté dans mon fait il n'est maille:
Maint d'entre-vous souvent juge au hazard,
Sans que pour ce tire à la courte-paille.

Tale about the Judge from Mesle

Pleading before a country magistrate,
Two lawyers would so cloud and obfuscate
A piddling point, that he, perplexed, could not
Say wherein lay the truth; whereon he got
Two straws—one short, one long—grasping them tight
(A grasping judge was he!). The long one fell
To the defendant, who, to his delight,
Was thus straightway exonerated. Well,
Imagine how the Court protests! "Do tell,"
Answers His Honor. "But I only do,
I daresay, just like all the rest of you!
Haphazardly, messieurs, you ply our laws:
The difference is, you guess and I draw straws."

Tale about the Judge from Mesle

Conte d'un paysan, qui avoit offensé son seigneur

Un Païsan son Seigneur offensa.
L'Histoire dit que c'estoit bagatelle:
Et toutesfois ce Seigneur le tança
Fort rudement; ce n'est chose nouvelle.
Coquin, dit-il, tu merites la hard:
Fay ton calcul d'y venir tost ou tard;
C'est une fin à tes pareils commune.
Mais je suis bon; et de trois peines l'une
Tu peux choisir. Ou de manger trente aulx,
J'entends sans boire, et sans prendre repos;
Ou de souffrir trente bons coups de gaules,
Bien appliquez sur tes larges épaules;
Ou de payer sur le champ cent écus.
Le Païsan consultant là-dessus:
Trente aulx sans boire! ah, dit-il en soy même,
Je n'appris onc à les manger ainsi.
De recevoir les trente coups aussi,
Je ne le puis sans un peril extrême.
Les cent écus c'est le pire de tous.
Incertain donc il se mit à genoux,
Et s'écria: Pour Dieu misericorde.
Son Seigneur dit: Qu'on apporte une corde;
Quoy le Galant m'ose répondre encor?
Le Païsan de peur qu'on ne le pende
Fait choix de l'ail; et le Seigneur commande
Que l'on en cueüille, et sur tout du plus fort.
Un aprés un luy-mesme il fait le conte:
Puis quand il void que son calcul se monte
A la trentaine, il les met dans un plat.

Tale about a Peasant Who Had Given His Lord Offense

There was a peasant once, whose impudence—
Of trifling sort, they tell us—nonetheless
Distressed his lord; who, taking much offense
Thereat, chastised him (as, alas *noblesse*
Is wont to do!) to harsh and cruel excess.
"Blackguard," he cried, "you ought to hang! And you
Most surely will, one day, as your kind do.
But kind am I, and mercy will I show you.
Three punishments I offer you; and so you
Freely may choose the one you wish. The first:
To swallow thirty garlic heads—without
A pause, that is, nor drink to slake your thirst.
The second: to be stoutly lashed about
The back and shoulders, thirty times. The third:
To pay me, here and now, a hundred crown."
Grégoire, the peasant, weighs his every word;
Reflects upon them, brow set in a frown:
"Eat thirty garlic heads, with nought to drink?"
He ponders. "Not one drop?... Oh, I don't think
I ever learned to eat them so! Nor would I
Fancy those thirty lashes, I'll be bound!
But pay a hundred crown? Good God, how should I?...
That one is far the worst!" And, knee to ground,
Doleful, he begs Monsieur; sighs many an "Ah!";
Cries: "Misery me!... *Misericordia!*..."
But Grand Seigneur ignores his plea, looks round,
And calls: "A noose!..." The rustic, fearing lest
He must be hanged, decides he would do best
To choose withal: "Well, garlic then." Thereat,
Our lord commands the bulbs be picked: big, fat,

Et cela fait le mal-heureux pied-plat
Prend le plus gros; en pitié le regarde;
Mange, et rechigne, ainsi que fait un chat
Dont les morceaux sont frotez de moûtarde.
Il n'oseroit de la langue y toucher.
Son Seigneur rit, et sur tout il prend garde
Que le Galant n'avale sans mascher.
Le premier passe; aussi fait le deuxiéme:
Au tiers il dit: Que le diable y ait part.
Bref il en fut à grand'peine au douziéme,
Que s'écriant: Haro la gorge m'ard
Tost, tost, dit-il, que l'on m'apporte à boire.
Son Seigneur dit: Ah ah, sire Gregoire,
Vous avez soif! je vois qu'en vos repas
Vous humectez volontiers le lampas.
Or beuvez donc; et beuvez à vostre aise:
Bon prou vous fasse: hola, du vin, hola.
Mais mon amy, qu'il ne vous en déplaise,
Il vous faudra choisir aprés cela
Des cent écus, ou de la bastonnade,
Pour suppléer au défaut de l'aillade.
—Qu'il plaise donc, dit l'autre, à vos bontez,
Que les aulx soient sur les coups precontez:
Car pour l'argent, par trop grosse est la somme:
Où la trouver moy qui suis un pauvre homme?
—Hé bien, souffrez les trente horions,
Dit le Seigneur; mais laissons les oignons.
Pour prendre cœur le Vassal en sa panse
Loge un long trait; se munit le dedans;
Puis souffre un coup avec grande constance.
Au deux il dit: Donnez-moy patience,

And hot! Ah yes, the hottest to the tongue!
Himself, he counts out thirty from among
The rest; sets out the lot. Grégoire inspects it;
Finds one—the biggest; woefully selects it...
Bites... Shudders in disgust... Grimaces (much
As cat will do with spice—mustard or such)...
Rejects it... Tries again... And, though he rues it,
Somehow he gets it down; but not before
Monsieur, amused, sees to it that he chews it,
And chews it well! The second even more
Scorches his gullet. Third, he swallows, crying:
"The Devil take these things!" In short, poor coz,
Reaching a dozen—God knows how he does!—
Stops, gags: "Enough! Enough! My throat... I'm dying!...
A drink!..." "What, friend? You thirst?" taunts lord, replying.
"Here! Take your favorite wine! Quaff all you will.
But, forthwith, after you have drunk your fill,
Still will you have to choose betwixt the two:
The lashing or the hundred crown. Nought less."
"Ah, but my lord, might I not hope that you,
With your good grace and gentle-heartedness,
Ought count the garlic I've already eaten
Against my thirty blows? For I'll be beaten
Rather than pay that price: too poor am I."
"Then thirty blows it is. Full thirty, hear?
Nought for the garlic!" snaps Monsieur, a sneer
Curling his callous lips. So, standing by,
The churl, disheartened by the harsh reply,
Swilling down one long draught—therewith to cheer
His heart and fill his gut—thus fortified,
Prepares for the attack upon his hide.
First blow: well borne. The second: "Ah! Sweet Jesus!"

Mon doux Jesus, en tous ces accidens.
Le tiers est rude, il en grince les dents,
Se courbe tout, et saute de sa place.
Au quart il fait une horrible grimace:
Au cinq un cri: mais il n'est pas au bout;
Et c'est grand cas s'il peut digerer tout.
On ne vit onc si cruelle avanture.
Deux forts paillards ont chacun un baston,
Qu'ils font tomber par poids et par mesure,
En observant la cadence et le ton.
Le mal-heureux n'a rien qu'une chanson.
Grace, dit-il: mais las! point de nouvelle;
Car le Seigneur fait frapper de plus belle,
Juge des coups, et tient sa gravité,
Disant toûjours qu'il a trop de bonté.
Le pauvre diable enfin craint pour sa vie.
Aprés vingt coups d'un ton piteux il crie:
Pour Dieu cessez: helas! je n'en puis plus.
Son Seigneur dit: Payez donc cent écus,
Net et contant: je sçais qu'à la desserre
Vous estes dur; j'en suis fasché pour vous.
Si tout n'est prest, vostre compere Pierre
Vous en peut bien assister entre nous.
Mais pour si peu vous ne vous feriez tondre.
Le mal-heureux n'osant presque répondre
Court au mugot, et dit: c'est tout mon fait.
On examine, on prend un trébuchet.
L'eau cependant luy coule de la face:
Il n'a point fait encor telle grimace.
Mais que luy sert? il convient tout payer.
C'est grand'pitié quand on fasche son maître!

He moans, "give me the strength…" But nothing eases
The awful pain. At length the third: he knits
His brow, arches his battered back, and grits
His teeth… The fourth: he lurches, and his face is
Contorted into horrible grimaces.
The fifth: a scream, a shriek, as well befits
The blow—with many yet to come; although
One wonders how he can withstand them so,
Unto the end of this most fell affair.
Two burly brutes with switches, hulking there,
Beat out a rhythmic cadence on his back,
Marking the measure with resounding "thwack,"
As he, poor boor, sings but one constant air:
"Mercy, monsieur…" But no, alas, alack!
Calling the tune, the lord is unrelenting,
Directing thus his minions twain, augmenting
Sempre crescendo his fortissimos;
Professing all the while his great good grace
And kindness at not doing worse. The blows
Rain on the peasant, one by one, apace,
Until, at twenty: "God above!" he groans,
And begs him cease, in woefulest of tones.
"Enough? A hundred crown then, on the spot!"
Replies the lord. "And nought less—not one jot—
Miserly wretch! That much you've got, and more!
Go fetch it all! Or find some creditor—
Pierre perhaps. Else for that paltry sum
Would you be flayed." The peasant now, struck dumb,
Ran, brought his bundle back, and humbly swore:
"I have but this." "Then pay it!" And he paid it.
And, as his lordship counted it and weighed it,
Grégoire, tormented yet more than before—

Ce Païsan eut beau s'humilier;
Et pour un fait, assez leger peut-estre,
Vuider la bourse, émoucher les épaules;
Sans qu'il luy fust dessus les cent écus,
Ny pour les aulx, ny pour les coups de gaules,
Fait seulement grace d'un carolus.

Sweat pouring from his brow—sorely repented
The wrong he did his lord. Mere bagatelle,
But error still. Oh, how he long lamented
The foul and hellish horrors that befell
His throat, his back, and (most of all!) his purse:
Throat burned, back whipped, purse bare! Distressed, distraught...
His fortune? Disappeared. And, what was worse,
That garlic and those lashes? All for nought.

Le Faiseur d'oreilles et le racommodeur de moules

Conte tiré des Cent Nouvelles Nouvelles, et d'un
Conte de Bocace

Sire Guillaume allant en marchandise,
Laissa sa femme, enceinte de six mois;
Simple, jeunette, et d'assez bonne guise,
Nommée Alix, du païs Champenois.
Compere André l'alloit voir quelquefois:
A quel dessein, besoin n'est de le dire,
Et Dieu le sçait: c'estoit un maistre sire;
Il ne tendoit guere en vain ses filets;
Ce n'estoit pas autrement sa coustume.
Sage eût esté l'oiseau qui de ses rets
Se fust sauvé sans laisser quelque plume.
Alix estoit fort neuve sur ce point.
Le trop d'esprit ne l'incommodoit point:
De ce défaut on n'accusoit la Belle.
Elle ignoroit les malices d'Amour.
La pauvre Dame alloit tout devant elle,
Et n'y sçavoit ny finesse ny tour.
Son mary donc se trouvant en emplete,
Elle au logis, en sa chambre seulette,
André survient, qui sans long compliment
La considere; et luy dit froidement:
Je m'ébahis comme au bout du Royaume
S'en est allé le Compere Guillaume,
Sans achever l'enfant que vous portez:
Car je vois bien qu'il luy manque une oreille:
Vostre couleur me le démontre assez,

The Ear-Smith and the
Mold-Repairer

Messire Guillaume, gone off to ply his trade,
Had left his wife at home, six months with child:
Alix by name, a Champenoise—young, mild,
Comely, but somewhat simple I'm afraid.
Often *compère* André would come to visit.
(Not necessary to say why, now is it?)
Lord knows, indeed a wily rogue was he.
Not one to set his traps for nought. Nay, never!
Clever must needs the rare bird be, whoever,
Caught in his snare or net, who yet can flee
Unplucked withal, her feathers all intact!
Artless in matters such, Alix, in fact,
Not much encumbered by excess of wit
(None would accuse the belle of that, I'm sure!),
Knew nothing of Love's fraud and counterfeit;
Nothing at all of mischievous Amour,
Of artful ruse, seductive stratagem,
Or of the devious cads that practice them.
Now, as I said, one day Messire Guillaume,
Taking his leave, had left his wife at home,
Up in her chamber, quite alone; when, there,
Who should appear? Our covetous *compère*.
With scarce a "How now?" or "Good day, madame,"
And gazing at her with a long, hard stare:
"I must confess," says he, "how shocked I am
To see Guillaume roam free, his sweet time taking,
Without first finishing the babe he's making.

En ayant veu mainte épreuve pareille.
—Bonté de Dieu! reprit-elle aussi-tost,
Que dites-vous? quoy d'un enfant monaût
J'accoucherois? n'y sçavez-vous remede?
—Si dea, fit-il, je vous puis donner aide
En ce besoin, et vous jureray bien,
Qu'autre que vous ne m'en feroit tant faire.
Le mal d'autruy ne me tourmente en rien;
Fors excepté ce qui touche au Compere:
Quant à ce point je m'y ferois mourir.
Or essayons, sans plus en discourir,
Si je suis maistre à forger des oreilles.
—Souvenez vous de les rendre pareilles,
Reprit la femme.—Allez, n'ayez soucy,
Repliqua-t-il, je prens sur moy cecy.
Puis le Galant montre ce qu'il sçait faire.
Tant ne fut nice (encor que nice fût)
Madame Alix, que le jeu ne luy plût.
Philosopher ne faut pour cette affaire.
André vaquoit de grande affection
A son travail; faisant ore un tendon,
Ore un reply, puis quelque cartilage;
Et n'y plaignant l'étofe et la façon.
Demain, dit-il, nous polirons l'ouvrage;
Puis le mettrons en sa perfection;
Tant et si bien qu'en ayez bonne issuë.
—Je vous en suis, dit-elle, bien tenuë:
Bon fait avoir icy bas un amy.
Le lendemain, pareille heure venuë,
Compere André ne fut pas endormy.
Il s'en alla chez la pauvre innocente.

For I can tell, it lacks an ear." "Monsieur?"
"Yes, plain as day... Your color shows... You see,
In this I'm something of a connoisseur..."
"Good God!" Alix exclaimed. "How can it be?
My child, one-eared?... Is there no remedy?"
"Well, yes... In fact, there is, now that you mention...
Come, let me give the matter my attention.
Mind you, I'd not do such for any other—
Others' concerns are no concern of mine!—
But help I shall. For how shall I decline
To succor you and dear Guillaume, my brother?
I'd sooner die, madame!... Well now, let's try.
Enough discussion... Come, let's see if I
Am not an ear-smith of the finest fettle."
"Take care to make them both the same!" "Aye, aye!
Leave that to me!" And, showing her his mettle,
Throwing himself into his work, impassioned,
He sets about to prove how ears are fashioned.
Now, simple though she be, Alix is not
So simple that she fails to take her pleasure.
(I'll not philosophize; you may, at leisure.)
Lest the unfinished ear be misbegot,
André, in turn, proceeds to give full measure,
Forming a tendon here, and there a fold,
A lobe, a cartilage... At length, "Behold,
Madame!" he cries. "The ear is almost done.
But not just yet... I'll come tomorrow. Then,
Setting about my labors once again,
I shall complete the task so well begun."
Says she: "Thank heaven for friends like you!" Next day,
Same hour, quite wide awake was our André.

Je viens, dit-il, toute affaire cessante,
Pour achever l'oreille que sçavez.
—Et moy, dit-elle, allois par un message
Vous avertir de haster cet ouvrage:
Montons en haut. Dés qu'ils furent montez,
On poursuivit la chose encommencée.
Tant fut ouvré, qu'Alix dans la pensée
Sur cette affaire un scrupule se mit;
Et l'innocente au bon apostre dit:
Si cet enfant avoit plusieurs oreilles,
Ce ne seroit à vous bien besogné.
—Rien, rien, dit-il, à cela j'ay soigné;
Jamais ne faux en rencontres pareilles.
Sur le métier l'oreille estoit encor,
Quand le mary revient de son voyage;
Caresse Alix, qui du premier abord:
Vous aviez fait, dit-elle, un bel ouvrage.
Nous en tenions sans le Compere André;
Et nostre enfant d'une oreille eust manqué.
Souffrir n'ay pû chose tant indecente.
Sire André donc, toute affaire cessante,
En a fait une: il ne faut oublier
De l'aller voir, et l'en remercier:
De tels amis on a toûjours affaire.
Sire Guillaume, au discours qu'elle fit,
Ne comprenant comme il se pouvoit faire
Que son Epouse eust eu si peu d'esprit,
Par plusieurs fois luy fit faire un recit
De tout le cas; puis outré de colere
Il prit une arme à costé de son lit;
Voulut tuer la pauvre Champenoise,

Flying posthaste to her of little wit,
"Madame, the ear..." he sighs. "Let's finish it."
And she, replying: "Yes, let's not delay.
Had you not come, I should have sent for you;
For there is yet, I fear, much work to do.
Come..." And they climb the stair, and recommence;
Working so hard that, in her innocence,
Alix, in time, conceives a doubt or two:
"Alack! What if my babe has several ears?
It seems to me you're making more than one."
"Nay, nay, madame. Not so. Allay your fears:
I know the ear-smith's trade second to none."
The ear was still a-making, still unfinished—
Despite André's endeavors undiminished—
When lo! Guillaume returns. His wife, straightway,
Responds to his caress: "Well, I must say!
A lovely baby you would have me bear!
One ear indeed! Imagine my despair!
One ear!... That is, save for Messire André.
Good friends like him, monsieur, are all too rare.
Lucky for me he made me one... I trust
You'll not forget to thank him." Piqued, nonplussed,
And much perplexed by her untoward confession,
Marveling at her guileless indiscretion,
Guillaume made her repeat—down to each tittle,
Each jot—every detail, the blasted lot;
Until, all fume and fuss, vexed not a little,
He knelt beside his bed and promptly got
His blunderbuss, to do her in; although
She had no notion what distressed him so,
And voiced dismay in proffering her defense.

Qui pretendoit ne l'avoir merité.
Son innocence et sa naïveté
En quelque sorte appaiserent la noise.
Helas Monsieur, dit la Belle en pleurant,
En quoy vous puis-je avoir fait du dommage?
Je n'ay donné vos draps ny vostre argent;
Le compte y est; et quant au demeurant,
André me dit quand il parfit l'enfant,
Qu'en trouveriez plus que pour vôtre usage:
Vous pouvez voir, si je mens tuez moy;
Je m'en rapporte à vostre bonne foy.
L'Epoux sortant quelque peu de colere,
Luy répondit: Or bien, n'en parlons plus;
On vous l'a dit, vous avez crû bien faire,
J'en suis d'accord, contester là-dessus
Ne produiroit que discours superflus:
Je n'ay qu'un mot. Faites demain en sorte
Qu'en ce logis j'attrape le Galant:
Ne parlez point de nostre different;
Soyez secrette, ou bien vous este morte.
Il vous le faut avoir adroitement;
Me feindre absent en un second voyage,
Et luy mander, par lettre ou par message,
Que vous avez à luy dire deux mots.
André viendra; puis de quelques propos
L'amuserez; sans toucher à l'oreille;
Car elle est faite, il n'y manque plus rien.
Notre innocente executa tres-bien
L'ordre donné; ce ne fut pas merveille;
La crainte donne aux bestes de l'esprit.
André venu, l'Epoux guere ne tarde,

Her innocence and utter naïveté
Tempered somewhat Guillaume's intransigence.

"Mercy, monsieur," she wept. "Tell me, I pray,
How have I done you ill? What harm is there?
Look! Count your linen... Count your silverware...
Your money... I gave none of it away...
Nothing is missing. See? Why, even he—
André—putting the final touches, swore
That now you had more than you'd bargained for.¹
See for yourself, I've done no injury.
Let monsieur kill me if he finds me lying."
Guillaume relents, considers, and, replying:
"Yes, quite..." says he. "The fault was not your own,
But our *compère's*—the wretch—and his alone.
We'll say no more: discussion serves no end.
One thing, however, would I have you do.
You must arrange another rendezvous,
Perforce, betwixt yourself and our fine friend.
Send him a messenger; a *billet doux*.
Pretend that I'm abroad again; that you
Must speak with him; that he must come tomorrow.
Yet let him not suspect that you and I
Have had our spat. Dissemble well, or die,
Madame! Fail at your peril and your sorrow.
For then would I most surely have to kill you.
Now when, at length, he comes—for come he will—you
Needs must amuse him with your idle chatter.
But mind you, no more talk about the ear!
That ear is finished. Perfect. Done. You hear?..."
Our innocent attended to the matter,
And rather well. (But that's no great surprise:

Monte, et fait bruit. Le compagnon regarde
Où se sauver: nul endroit il ne vit,
Qu'une ruelle en laquelle il se mit.
Le mary frappe; Alix ouvre la porte;
Et de la main fait signe incontinent,
Qu'en la ruelle est caché le Galant.
Sire Guillaume estoit armé de sorte
Que quatre Andrez n'auroient pû l'étonner.
Il sort pourtant, et va querir main forte,
Ne le voulant sans doute assassiner;
Mais quelque oreille au pauvre homme couper:
Peut-estre pis, ce qu'on coupe en Turquie,
Pays cruel et plein de barbarie.
C'est ce qu'il dit à sa femme tout bas:
Puis l'emmena sans qu'elle osast rien dire;
Ferma tres-bien la porte sur le sire.
André se crût sorti d'un mauvais pas,
Et que l'Epoux ne sçavoit nulle chose.
Sire Guillaume en révant à son cas
Change d'avis, en soy-mesme propose
De se vanger avecque moins de bruit,
Moins de scandale, et beaucoup plus de fruit.
Alix, dit-il, allez querir la femme
De sire André; contez-luy vostre cas
De bout en bout; courez, n'y manquez pas.
Pour l'amener vous direz à la Dame
Que son mary court un peril tres-grand;
Que je vous ay parlé d'un chastiment
Qui la regarde, et qu'aux faiseurs d'oreilles
On fait souffrir en rencontres pareilles:
Chose terrible, et dont le seul penser

Terror, it seems, can turn the witless wise.)
André appears as planned. Then, with a clatter,
Up the stair stamps Guillaume. The would-be lover
Looks right, looks left, hoping he might discover
Some place to run; finds none; and must, instead,
Take refuge there between the wall and bed.
The husband knocks. Alix flings wide the door,
Points to the hiding place. Guillaume, indeed,
Is so well armed that even were there four
Andrés he would have precious little need
To be alarmed. Yet out he goes; no doubt
Intent on doing less than kill the lout:
Keen, I suppose, on lopping off his ear.
(Or even worse: what the barbaric Turk
Cuts off to show the world his handiwork!)
At any rate, our vengeance-bent *messire*,
Whispering to his wife, led her outside
And tightly shut the door. Much gratified,
André assumed Guillaume knew nought, and thought
He had succeeded in not getting caught.
Meanwhile Guillaume, judging the situation,
Changes his mind, hits on a vengeance sweeter:
One that will spare him much humiliation,
And that, as vengeance ought, will cheat the cheater.
"Madame Alix"—thus he commands—"I bid
You find the wife of sire André. Relate
In full detail precisely what he did.
Tell her I've caught and pent the reprobate;
That for his good—and hers!—she'd best betake her
Here, and without delay, lest our ear-maker
Suffer a frightful woe; that she, his mate,

Vous fait dresser les cheveux à la teste;
Que son Epoux est tout prest d'y passer;
Qu'on n'attend qu'elle afin d'estre à la feste.
Que toutesfois, comme elle n'en peut mais,
Elle pourra faire changer la peine:
Amenez-la, courez; je vous promets
D'oublier tout moyennant qu'elle vienne.
Madame Alix, bien joyeuse s'en fut
Chez sire André dont la femme accourut
En diligence, et quasi hors d'haleine;
Puis monta seule, et ne voyant André,
Crut qu'il estoit quelque part enfermé.
Comme la Dame estoit en ces alarmes,
Sire Guillaume ayant quitté ses armes
La fait asseoir, et puis commence ainsi:
L'ingratitude est mere de tout vice.
André m'a fait un notable service;
Parquoy, devant que vous sortiez d'icy,
Je luy rendray si je puis la pareille.
En mon absence il a fait une oreille
Au fruit d'Alix: je veux d'un si bon tour
Me revancher, et je pense une chose:
Tous vos enfans ont le nez un peu court:
Le moule en est asseurément la cause.
Or je les sçais des mieux raccommoder.
Mon avis donc est que sans retarder
Nous pourvoyions de ce pas à l'affaire.
Disant ces mots, il vous prend la Commere,
Et prés d'André la jetta sur le lit,
Moitié raisin, moitié figue en jouït.
La Dame prit le tout en patience;

And she alone, can save him from his fate.
Else is his villainy retaliated,
And he, in brief, forthwith abbreviated!
Run, woman. Bring her here. For, if you fetch her,
Then shall your erstwhile dalliance with the lecher
Be pardoned and forgotten." Much elated,
Madame Alix ran off to André's house,
Brought back a terrified and breathless spouse,
Who, growing each moment more and more alarmed,
Climbing the stair alone, looked vainly round
In hopes to find her husband; but who found
None but Messire Guillaume. He, now unarmed,
Bade her be seated and addressed her thus:
"Ingratitude, madame, is infamy.
Never, I vow, will it be said that we
Fail to repay the favors done to us.
Compère André did such a one, for me,
That shall not go unmatched. Indeed, here, now,
Shall I reciprocate. You ask: 'And how?'
Well, in my absence, in this very room,
He forged an ear in my Alix's womb.
Now then, your children—I seem to recall—
Are all possessed of noses much too small.
The mold in which they're cast, one must assume,
Is cause of that defect. But, with my skill,
I can repair the flaw and cure the ill.
Best we begin at once." So saying, unbidden,
He threw her to the bed, near where Monsieur,
Cringing beneath, had all the while lain hidden,
And, willy-nilly, did his will with her.
Bearing with patience his assaults, she blessed

Benit le Ciel de ce que la vengeance
Tomboit sur elle, et non sur sire André;
Tant elle avoit pour luy de charité.
Sire Guillaume estoit de son costé
Si fort émeu, tellement irrité,
Qu'à la pauvrette il ne fit nulle grace
Du Talion, rendant à son Epoux
Féves pour pois, et pain blanc pour foüace.
Qu'on dit bien vray que se venger est doux!
Tres-sage fut d'en user de la sorte:
Puis qu'il vouloit son honneur reparer,
Il ne pouvoit mieux que par cette porte
D'un tel affront à mon sens se tirer.
André vit tout, et n'osa murmurer;
Jugea des coups; mais ce fut sans rien dire;
Et loüa Dieu que le mal n'estoit pire.
Pour une oreille il auroit composé.
Sortir à moins c'estoit pour luy merveilles:
Je dis à moins; car mieux vaut, tout prisé,
Cornes gagner que perdre ses oreilles.

The heavens above—such was her charity!—
That she and not her hapless spouse should be
Butt of the wrong thus rightfully redressed.
Guillaume, in turn, so wrathful, so distressed,
Granting her little quarter for all that,
Pressed boldly on, as then and there he gave
An ample share of tit for André's tat,
Wreaking his sweet revenge upon the knave.
(For eye, an eye; for tooth, a tooth; and nose,
Forsooth, for ear, thereat. For so it goes.)
Wise was Guillaume, in truth, thus to exact
Full measure for his honor thus attacked.
No better way than this: André, poor sot,
Saw every thrust and parry, but dared not
Utter a word. Instead, he praised the Lord
That he, in fact, escaped unscathed, unscored.
He would have settled for an ear or so,
And borne misfortune like a *philosophe*.
But better this; for rather would man grow
A pair of horns than have his ears cut off.

The Ear-Smith and the Mold-Repairer

La Servante justifiée.

Nouvelle tirée des Contes de la Reine de Navarree

Bocace n'est le seul qui me fournit.
Je vas par fois en une autre boutique.
Il est bien vray que ce divin esprit
Plus que pas un me donne de pratique.
Mais comme il faut manger de plus d'un pain,
Je puise encore en un vieux magazin;
Vieux, des plus vieux, où Nouvelles Nouvelles
Sont jusqu'à cent, bien déduites et belles
Pour la pluspart, et de tres-bonne main.
Pour cette fois la Reine de Navarre,
D'un c'estoit moy naïf autant que rare,
Entretiendra dans ces Vers le Lecteur.
Voicy le fait, quiconque en soit l'Auteur.
J'y mets du mien selon les occurrences:
C'est ma coustume; et sans telles licences
Je quitterois la charge de conteur.
Un homme donc avoit belle servante.
Il la rendit au jeu d'Amour sçavante.
Elle estoit fille à bien armer un lit,
Pleine de suc, et donnant appetit;
Ce qu'on appelle en François bonne robbe.
Par un beau jour cet homme se dérobe
D'avec sa femme; et d'un tres-grand matin
S'en va trouver sa Servante au jardin.
Elle faisoit un bouquet pour Madame:
C'estoit sa feste. Voyant donc de la femme
Le bouquet fait, il commence à loüer
L'assortîment; tâche à s'insinüer:
S'insinüer en fait de Chambriere,

The Servant-Girl Exonerated

Divine Boccaccio![1] That most eminent
Of raconteurs! The one whom I frequent
More than the rest. Yet others too are there—
Purveyors of a no-less-worthy ware—
With whom I do my trade. For, as we say,
Best not to eat the same bread every day,
But rather, now and then, taste different fare.
Thus, often, do I shop at that old store—
One of the oldest—with its full fivescore
Nouvelles of so-called "novel" fabrication:
Well crafted, for the most part, and replete
With elegant and humorous narration.[2]
Today, however, is Queen Marguerite,
Late of Navarre, my inspiration; whose
Innocent "That was me!" will much amuse.[3]
(Still, author though she be, I think it meet
That I admit my part: the skill I use
To tell her tale—the bit I add, delete...
To wit, such liberties as well befit it.
Else what would be my storyteller's art?
No art at all, and I would gladly quit it.)
Well now, my tale, if you permit... It
Tells of the ruse of man who lost his heart
To maid. But married swain was he; and she,
A servant-girl, buxom as belle should be—
Succulent-fleshed: a proper *beau morceau*,
As some would say, well fit for bed.[4] And he,
Well fit to teach her all she had to know
Of love's delights, was quick to teach her so!
One morning, with his wife asleep beside him,

C'est proprement couler sa main au sein:
Ce qui fut fait. La Servante soudain
Se défendit: mais de quelle maniere?
Sans rien gaster: c'estoit une façon
Sur le marché; bien sçavoit sa leçon.
La Belle prend les fleurs qu'elle avoit mises
En un monceau, les jette au Compagnon.
Il la baisa pour en avoir raison:
Tant et si bien qu'ils en vinrent aux prises.
En cet étrif la Servante tomba.
Luy d'en tirer aussi-tost avantage.
Le mal-heur fut que tout ce beau ménage
Fut découvert d'un logis prés de là.
Nos gens n'avoient pris garde à cette affaire.
Une voisine apperceut le mystere.
L'Epoux la vit, je ne sçais pas comment.
Nous voila pris, dit-il à sa Servante.
Nostre voisine est languarde et méchante.
Mais ne soyez en crainte aucunement.
Il va trouver sa femme en ce moment:
Puis fait si bien que s'estant éveillée
Elle se leve; et sur l'heure habillée,
Il continuë à joüer son rollet:
Tant qu'à dessein d'aller faire un bouquet,
La pauvre Epouse au jardin est menée.
Là fut par luy procedé de nouveau.
Mesme debat, mesme jeu se commence.
Fleurs de voler; tetons d'entrer en danse.
Elle y prit goust; le jeu luy sembla beau.
Somme, que l'herbe en fut encor froissée.

Stealthily our monsieur arose and hied him
Out to the garden, where he spied his prize
Amongst the flowers, there tressing a bouquet
To fete Madame. (Her birthday was that day.)
Slyly he heaps his praise, in scheming wise,
Upon her nosegay; casts his lustful eyes
Over her body, seeking how he best
Might curry favor... Now, ofttimes caressed,
A serving-wench's favor is best curried
With hand slipped, unassuming and unhurried,
Into the bosom, square upon the breast.
So will he do. And so will she protest—
Weakly, withal!—against said bust-aggressor,
Thrusting a fistful of her petals at him,
As he, with parrying hug and kiss, will press her;
Till, with nor will nor courage to combat him,
Onto the grass she falls, with him upon her.
As thus they frolic, trifling with her honor—
Reckless their gay abandon, come what may!—
A neighbor lady, prying, eyes their play.
"Alas," cries he, seeing her spying, "now
Are we observed! That witch is sure to prattle.
But have no fear: I'll find a way somehow
To save the day." And so, girding for battle,
Back to his wife he goes; wakes her; suggests
She come pick flowers. She, not quite sure what for,
Follows him to the garden, where, once more,
He plays love's game. The same: buds flying, breasts
A-bobble and a-bounce... Madame, in short,

La pauvre Dame alla l'apresdînée
Voir sa voisine, à qui ce secret là
Chargeoit le cœur: elle se soulagea
Tout dés l'abord: Je ne puis, ma commere,
Dit cette femme avec un front severe,
Laisser passer sans vous en avertir
Ce que j'ay veu. Voulez-vous vous servir
Encor long-temps d'une fille perduë?
A coups de pied, si j'estois que de vous,
Je l'envoyrois ainsi qu'elle est venuë.
Comment! elle est aussi brave que nous.
Or bien, je sçais celuy de qui procede
Cette piafe: apportez-y remede
Tout au plustost: car je vous avertis
Que ce matin estant à la fenestre,
(Ne sçais pourquoy) j'ay veu de mon logis
Dans son jardin vostre mary paroistre,
Puis la Galande; et tous deux se sont mis
A se jetter quelques fleurs à la teste.
Sur ce propos l'autre l'arresta coy.
Je vous entends, dit-elle, c'estoit moy.

LA VOISINE

Voire! écoutez le reste de la feste:
Vous ne sçavez où je veux en venir.
Les bonnes gens se sont pris à cueillir
Certaines fleurs que baisers on appelle.

LA FEMME

C'est encor moy que vous preniez pour elle.

Rumples the grass no less than did the maid,
And takes, in fact, much pleasure in the sport.
Later that day, as was her wont, she paid
A visit to her neighbor's house. The latter—
Whose secret weighed upon her, heavily—
Unable to resist, began to chatter
About what she had seen, blathering at her:
"Your maid... That jade! If she were mine... Ah me!
Commère, that slut would straightway surely be
Sent flying with a kick!" "Why, what's the matter?
I find her quite as proper, friend, as us."
"Then shame on you that you should find her thus!
Listen to what I saw that hussy do:
This very morning, at my window, I
Was gazing aimlessly—I know not why—
When suddenly Monsieur came into view;
And then, next moment, she—that trollop!—too,
Both throwing flowers each at the other." "Oh?
I understand," Madame replied. "I know!
Friend, you need go no farther: that was me."

THE NEIGHBOR

You? Hardly! Hear me out: I've more to tell.
Such were the flowers they plucked that, presently,
Your husband and your "proper" *demoiselle*
Exchanged the blooms upon each other's lips:
They kissed!

THE WIFE

        No, that was me you took for her.

LA VOISINE

Du jeu des fleurs à celuy des tetons
Ils sont passez: aprés quelques façons
A pleine main l'on les a laissez prendre.

LA FEMME

Et pourquoy non? c'estoit moy: vostre Epoux
N'a-t-il pas donc les mesmes droits sur vous?

LA VOISINE

Cette personne enfin sur l'herbe tendre
Est trebuchée, et, comme je le croy,
Sans se blesser; vous riez?

LA FEMME

        C'estoit moy.

LA VOISINE

Un cotillon a paré la verdure.

LA FEMME

C'estoit le mien.

LA VOISINE

     Sans vous mettre en courroux:
Qui le portoit de la fille ou de vous?
C'est là le point: car Monsieur vostre Epoux
Jusques au bout a poussé l'avanture.

THE NEIGHBOR

When they had done with flowers, then did Monsieur
Pass to her breasts, fondling their tender tips
And all the rest, to heart's content.

THE WIFE

                                        Why not?
I told you, that was me he fondled. What?
Would you, *commère*, not let your husband, too,
Do what he would, and when he likes, with you?

THE NEIGHBOR

Soon she was falling, sprawling on the ground.
But was she hurt? Not likely, I'll be bound!
Not from that fall!... You laugh?

THE WIFE

                                  Yes. That was me.

THE NEIGHBOR

A moment later, and what came to pass?
A petticoat lay flung upon the grass!

THE WIFE

Yes. It was mine, that petticoat.

THE NEIGHBOR

                              I see...
Your petticoat... Aha... But, tell me, friend...
The question is—not meaning to offend—
Which of you had it on? You or the lass?
Because, if you forgive my saying so,
Your husband went as far as he could go.

LA FEMME

Qui? c'estoit moy: vostre teste est bien dure.

LA VOISINE

Ah; c'est assez. Je ne m'informe plus:
J'ay pourtant l'œil assez bon ce me semble:
J'aurois juré que je les avois veus
En ce lieu-là se divertir ensemble.
Mais excusez; et ne la chassez pas.

LA FEMME

Pourquoy chasser? j'en suis tres-bien servie.

LA VOISINE

Tant pis pour vous: c'est justement le cas.
Vous en tenez, ma commere m'amie.

THE WIFE

Blockhead! I told you... That was me! I know! [5]

THE NEIGHBOR

Oh? Then I'll say no more, *commère*. Excuse me.
Doubtless you think my eyes must much abuse me.
But I know what I see and when I see it!
I could have sworn that she... I guarantee it!
But you'll not send her packing!

THE WIFE

                            Packing? Fie!
Why? None, I vow, is better served than I.

THE NEIGHBOR

So much the worse for you, my friend! So be it.

Le Calendrier des vieillards

Nouvelle tirée de Bocace

Plus d'une fois je me suis étonné,
Que ce qui fait la paix du mariage
En est le poinct le moins consideré,
Lors que l'on met une fille en ménage.
Les pere et mere ont pour objet le bien;
Tout le surplus, ils le comptent pour rien;
Jeunes tendrons à Vieillards apparient.
Et cependant je voy qu'ils se soucient
D'avoir chevaux à leur char attelez
De mesme taille, et mesmes chiens couplez:
Ainsi des bœufs, qui de force pareille
Sont toûjours pris: car ce seroit merveille
Si sans cela la charruë alloit. bien.
Comment pourroit celle du mariage
Ne mal aller, estant un attelage
Qui bien souvent ne se rapporte en rien?
J'en vas conter un exemple notable.
On sçait qui fut Richard de Quinzica,
Qui mainte Feste à sa femme allegua,
Mainte vigile, et maint jour feriable,
Et du devoir crut s'échaper par là.
Tres-lourdement il erroit en cela.
Cestuy Richard estoit Juge dans Pise,
Homme sçavant en l'étude dex loix,
Riche d'ailleurs; mais dont la barbe grise
Monstroit assez qu'il devoit faire choix
De quelque femme à peu prés de même âge;
Ce qu'il ne fit, prenant en mariage
La mieux seante, et la plus jeune d'ans

The Greybeards' Calendar

Often am I appalled, I must confess,
By those who selfishly will trade away
Their marriageable daughters' happiness.
What matters most, and what brings most success
To married life, is what such parents pay
The least attention to! Their only thought
Is gain. Their daughters are not wed, but bought.
They mate their fledgling virgins, shamelessly,
With rich old men. Yet will they take great care
To see their horses bridled as a pair,
Their hounds well coupled; and to guarantee
Their oxen both of equal strength. For how,
Otherwise, would they do to pull the plough?
Well, by that token, one ought likewise see
The marriage-plough well paired. How should it be
Properly drawn when, yoked for the endeavor,
Spouses have nought in common whatsoever?
Which brings me to my tale. It tells about
Richard de Quinzica—a noted name,
One that the gentle reader knows, no doubt:[1]
A judge in Pisa; but who owes his fame
Not to his wealth or judgely acumen,
But to a calendar of his invention,
Cluttered with dates demanding man's abstention
From husbandly pursuit. Time and again
Some holy office—vigil, mass, or such—
Gave him much pious pretext not to touch
Madame his wife. In truth, one long "amen"
Replaced the pleasures of the bed. But he,

De la Cité, fille bien alliée,
Belle sur tout; c'estoit Bartholomée
De Galandi, qui parmy ses parens
Pouvoit compter les plus gros de la ville.
En ce ne fit Richard tour d'homme habile:
Et l'on disoit communément de luy,
Que ses enfans ne manqueroient de peres.
Tel fait mestier de conseiller autruy,
Qui ne voit goute en ses propres affaires.
Quinzica donc n'ayant dequoy servir
Un tel oiseau qu'estoit Bartholomée,
Pour s'excuser, et pour la contenir,
Ne rencontroit point de jour en l'année,
Selon son compte, et son Calendrier,
Où l'on se pûst sans scrupule appliquer
Au fait d'Hymen; chose aux vieillards commode;
Mais dont le sexe abhorre la methode.
Quand je dis point, je veux dire tres-peu:
Encor ce peu luy donnoit de la peine.
Toute en feries il mettoit la semaine;
Et bien souvent faisoit venir en jeu
Saint qui ne fut jamais dans la legende.
Le Vendredy, disoit-il, nous demande
D'autres pensers, ainsi que chacun sçait:
Pareillement il faut que l'on retranche
Le Samedy, non sans juste sujet,
Dautant que c'est la veille du Dimanche.
Pour ce dernier, c'est un jour de repos.
Quant au Lundy, je ne trouve à propos
De commencer par ce poinct la semaine;
Ce n'est le fait d'une ame bien Chrestienne.

Clever or no, was not to go scot-free,
For all his store of lore and erudition.
As for Madame, your obvious supposition—
Given her greybeard mate—would be that she
Must be of equal years, grizzled no less.
Alas, not so! It was Bartholomée
De Galandi—creature of comeliness,
Young offspring of a house most *distinguée*,
Fairest by far of all the fairest Pisans—
That he had chosen for his wife. I need
Hardly put forward all the many reasons
Why such a choice was dangerous indeed!
"Their children won't be lacking fathers, surely!"
Quipped his compatriots, none too obscurely
(Though most would do the same, I must assume).
Thus, though endowed with wealth and years, our groom,
Without one sou of love's hard currency,
Has nought to pay his bride, sweet bird of youth;
And, to excuse his lack, bending the truth,
He twists the calendar to such degree
That he convinces her no decent day
For man-and-wifely folderol exists,
Insisting that one pure of heart resists.
(Old men nod "Aye!" Wives sigh a sullen "Nay!")
Now, when I tell you "nought," I ought to say,
Rather, "a little." Still, that little spent him.
Wherefore he thought it meet—the lustless sophist—
To vow that every day was holy-officed,
Vouched to its saint. (Even should he invent him!)
Thus was the week passed in divine review:
"Friday," said he, "demands much contemplation.
Saturday is no proper time thereto,

Les autres jours autrement s'excusoit:
Et quand venoit aux festes solemnelles,
C'estoit alors que Richard triomphoit,
Et qu'il donnoit les leçons les plus belles.
Long-temps devant toûjours il s'abstenoit,
Long-temps aprés il en usoit de même;
Aux Quatre-temps autant il en faisoit;
Sans oublier l'Avent ny le Carême.
Cette saison pour le Vieillard estoit
Un temps de Dieu, jamais ne s'en lassoit.
De Patrons mesme il avoit une liste.
Point de quartier pour un Evangeliste,
Pour un Apostre, ou bien pour un Docteur:
Vierge n'estoit, Martyr, et Confesseur
Qu'il ne chommast; tous les sçavoit par cœur.
Que s'il estoit au bout de son scrupule,
Il alleguoit les jours malencontreux;
Puis les broüillars, et puis la canicule,
De s'excuser n'estant jamais honteux.
La chose ainsi presque toûjours égale,
Quatre fois l'an, de grace speciale,
Nostre Docteur regaloit sa moitié,
Petitement; enfin c'estoit pitié.
A cela prés, il traitoit bien sa femme.
Les affiquets, les habits à changer,
Joyaux, bijoux, ne manquoient à la Dame;
Mais tout cela n'est que pour amuser
Un peu de temps des esprits de poupée;
Droit au solide alloit Bartholomée.
Son seul plaisir dans la belle saison,
C'estoit d'aller à certaine maison

Being so close to Sunday's adoration
And soul's repose. For Monday, one might deem
That to begin the week therewith would seem
No Christian thing to do." And on and on
He goes: the rest are no less frowned upon.
Come holy feasts, our chaste pontificator
Gives proof triumphant of a zeal still greater,
For weeks before, and weeks and weeks anon,
Refraining from the pleasures of the flesh.
Come fasts as well, and he affirms afresh
Good reasons for remaining abstinent:
Ember Days, Advent... Not to mention Lent,
God's holiest of seasons. As for saints,
His list was long: for each, the same constraints.
Likewise for every Father of the Church,
Virgin, evangelist, martyr, confessor...
He knew them all by heart, each intercessor,
And took the greatest care lest he besmirch
Their honor with the carnal act. And when
No holiday or saint, greater or lesser,
Came quick to mind to spare his virtue, then,
Reaching the end of his canonic tether,
He would protest the inauspicious weather—
The rain, the fog, the dog-day heat, the cold...
Any excuse indeed would do. In sum,
All things considered, if the truth be told,
Four times a year, at most, could he succumb
To passion's call. And then not much at all,
Nor very well; in fact, rather pathetic,
The efforts of our elderly ascetic.
Yet, save for that defect, Monsieur, withal,
Dealt kindly with Madame; bestowed upon her

Que son mary possedoit sur la coste:
Ils y couchoient tous les huit jours sans faute.
Là quelquefois sur la mer ils montoient,
Et le plaisir de la pesche goustoient,
Sans s'éloigner que bien peu de la rade.
Arrive donc, qu'un jour de promenade,
Bartholomée et Messer le Docteur,
Prennent chacun une barque à Pescheur,
Sortent sur mer; ils avoient fait gageure
A qui des deux auroit plus de bon-heur,
Et trouveroit la meilleure avanture
Dedans sa pesche, et n'avoient avec eux,
Dans chaque barque, en tout qu'un homme ou deux.
Certain Corsaire apperceut la chaloupe
De nostre Epouse, et vint avec sa troupe
Fondre dessus; l'emmena bien et beau;
Laissa Richard: soit que prés du rivage
Il n'osast pas hazarder davantage;
Soit qu'il craignist qu'ayant dans son vaisseau
Nostre Vieillard, il ne pût de sa proye
Si bien joüir; car il aimoit la joye
Plus que l'argent, et toûjours avoit fait
Avec honneur son mestier de Corsaire;
Au jeu d'Amour estoit homme d'effet,
Ainsi que sont gens de pareille affaire.
Gens de mer sont toûjours prests à bien faire,
Ce qu'on appelle autrement bons garçons:
On n'en voit point qui les festes allegue.
Or tel estoit celuy dont nous parlons,
Ayant pour nom Pagamin de Monegue.
La Belle fit son devoir de pleurer

Many a generous gift; lavishing on her
Trinkets that might delight a mindless doll—
Finery, baubles, costly jewel and gem.
But soon Bartholomée would tire of them
And seek more solid and enduring pleasure.
Now, every spring the couple took their leisure
Off by the sea, one day a week or so,
Sailing and fishing, never far from shore.
One evening, as they ventured out *sur l'eau*,
In separate skiffs, casting their lines, each swore,
In jest, to best the other and catch more
And better fish. And there they are, when, oh!
Horrors! a corsair and his pirate troop
Spy the fair spouse adrift, and straightway swoop
Down on her bark and sweep her off; with never
A thought to snatch the old man too, however.
Either because the risk was great—Monsieur
Hugged close to shore—or, as you may infer,
Because our corsair felt his presence might,
Indeed, impede the plans he had for her:
To wit, to dally to his heart's delight.
For joy and frolic, more than money, were
The object of his sport. Despite his trade
He was a good and gallant sort, who played
The pirate's part with courteous, honest air,
Typical of such folk as ply the seas.
A lover first and foremost: debonair,
Forthright and frank; unlike your devotees
Who find some saint to worship every day!
Well, Pagamin de Monègue, as I say
(So was he called), was such a man as that.

Un demy jour, tant qu'il se put étendre:
Et Pagamin de la reconforter;
Et nostre Epouse à la fin de se rendre.
Il la gagna; bien sçavoit son mestier.
Amour s'en mit, Amour ce bon apôtre,
Dix mille fois plus Corsaire que l'autre,
Vivant de rapt, faisant peu de quartier.
La Belle avoit sa rançon toute preste:
Tres-bien luy prit d'avoir dequoy payer;
Car là n'estoit ny vigile ny Feste.
Elle oublia ce beau Calendrier
Rouge par tout, et sans nul jour ouvrable:
De la ceinture on le luy fit tomber;
Plus n'en fut fait mention qu'à la table.
Nostre Legiste eust mis son doigt au feu
Que son Epouse estoit toûjours fidele,
Entiere, et chaste; et que moyennant Dieu
Pour de l'argent on luy rendroit la Belle.
De Pagamin il prit un sauf-conduit,
L'alla trouver, luy mit la carte-blanche.
Pagamin dit: Si je n'ay pas bon bruit,
C'est à grand tort: je veux vous rendre franche,
Et sans rançon, vostre chere moitié.
Ne plaise à Dieu que si belle amitié
Soit par mon fait de desastre ainsi pleine.
Celle pour qui vous prenez tant de peine
Vous reviendra selon vostre desir.
Je ne veux point vous vendre ce plaisir.
Faites-moy voir seulement qu'elle est vôtre;
Car si j'allois vous en rendre quelque autre,
Comme il m'en tombe assez entre les mains,

Now, when said buccaneer abducts said beauty,
The latter goes about her wifely duty,
Shedding a half-day's worth of tears thereat.
With comforting caress our hero dries
Her eyes; as less and less milady cries,
And more and more relents; until she is—
To put the matter delicately—his.
He knew his trade. (Though Love, that hypocrite—
A thousand times more pirate, he, the knave!—
Did his part, too, to make the most of it.)
Madame knew what the ransom was to save
Her skin, and had no qualms to pay the price.
The which she did, unfretting and unfettered—
No patron claimed this day in Paradise!—
Delighted, at long last, to sacrifice
That calendar and all its dates red-lettered!
Loosed from her girdle, where, forsooth, she kept it,
They dropped it to the floor and forthwith swept it
Under the rug, to speak of it no more.
Meanwhile, our judge, lamenting on the shore,
Swore up and down that her fidelity,
Honor, and chastity could not be shaken;
That, with God's help—and money promptly paid—
She would return, unsullied and unstrayed.
At length he asks that he be safely taken
By escort to the corsair's boat; whereby
Judge pleads his case. Says pirate in reply:
"My friend, I ill deserve the fame I bear—
Ill fame, I fear—and I would heed your prayer
And set her free. For, heaven forfend that I
Bring foul misfortune to a love so fair.

Ce me seroit une espece de blâme.
Ces jours passez je pris certaine Dame,
Dont les cheveux sont quelque peu chastains,
Grande de taille, en bon poinct, jeune, et fraische.
Si cette Belle aprés vous avoir veu
Dit estre à vous, c'este autant de conclu:
Reprenez-la: rien ne vous en empêche.
Richard reprit: Vous parlez sagement:
Et me traitez trop genereusement.
De son mestier il faut que chacun vive.
Mettez un prix à la pauvre captive,
Je le payray contant, sans hesiter.
Le compliment n'est icy necessaire:
Voilà ma bourse, il ne faut que compter.
Ne me traitez que comme on pourroit faire
En pareil cas l'homme le moins connu.
Seroit-il dit que vous m'eussiez vaincu
D'honnesteté? non sera sur mon ame.
Vous le verrez. Car, quant à cette Dame,
Ne doutez point qu'elle ne soit à moy.
Je ne veux pas que vous m'ajoûtiez foy,
Mais aux baisers que de la pauvre femme
Je recevray, ne craignant qu'un seul poinct:
C'est qu'à me voir de joye elle ne meure.
On fait venir l'Epouse tout à l'heure,
Qui froidement et ne s'émouvant point,
Devant ses yeux voit son mary paroistre,
Sans témoigner seulement le connoistre,
Non plus qu'un homme arrivé du Perou.
Voyez, dit-il, la pauvrette est honteuse
Devant les gens; et sa joye amoureuse

Your wish is granted, and I shall deliver
Madame forthwith. But, sire, before I give her—
Not sell her, mind you!—first must I be sure
Which one is yours; which, of my store, is who
You say she is. For it would never do
To give you someone else's *bel amour*,
Now would it!" Wherewith he proceeds to tell
The virtues and the beauties of the belle:
Ample of stature, full and firm of flesh,
Chestnut of hair, well-favored, young and fresh...
"If such be yours, then, when she comes and sees you,
Let her but thus declare; and, may it please you,
So may you leave and freely take her." "Ah,"
Sighing, replies Richard de Quinzica.
"I much appreciate the guarantees you
Offer in good and generous wise. But, truly,
All of us ply our trades; and you, no less.
So let my reputation not impress,
Nor my importance cower you unduly.
My purse is yours: bested I shall not be
In goodliness and generosity.
As for the lady, sire, you need not doubt me:
My wife is she. The proof? When I appear,
Watch how she runs and flings her arms about me,
Hugging and kissing. Why, my only fear
Is lest she die of joy!" The wife arrives,
Looks, sees her husband standing there: survives...
Coldly she gazes on him, staring blankly,
Unknowingly, as if His Judgeship, frankly,
Had fallen from the moon.[2] "You see?" he sighs,
"How overcome she is. Yet will she, here,

N'ose éclater: soyez seur qu'à mon cou,
Si j'estois seul, elle seroit sautée.
Pagamin dit: Qu'il ne tienne à cela:
Dedans sa chambre allez, conduisez-la.
Ce qui fut fait: et la chambre fermée;
Richard commence: Et là, Bartholomée,
Comme tu fais! je suis ton Quinzica,
Toûjours le mesme à l'endroit de sa femme.
Regarde-moy. Trouves-tu, ma chere ame,
En mon visage un si grand changement!
C'est la douleur de ton enlevement
Qui me rend tel; et toy seule en es cause.
T'ay-je jamais refusé nulle chose,
Soit pour ton jeu, soit pour tes vestemens?
En estoit-il quelqu'une de plus brave?
De ton vouloir ne me rendois-je esclave?
Tu le seras estant avec ces gens.
Et ton honneur, que crois-tu qu'il devienne?
—Ce qu'il pourra, répondit brusquement
Bartholomée. Est-il temps maintenant
D'en avoir soin? s'en est-on mis en peine,
Quand malgré moy l'on m'a jointe avec vous?
Vous vieux penard, moy fille jeune et drüe,
Qui meritois d'estre un peu mieux pourveüe,
Et de gouster ce qu'Hymen a de doux.
Pour cet effet j'estois assez aimable;
Et me trouvois aussi digne, entre nous,
De ces plaisirs, que j'en estois capable.
Or est le cas allé d'autre façon.
J'ay pris mary qui pour toute chanson
N'a jamais eu que ses jours de ferie;

Come kiss me not, before your prying eyes,
Too coy to let love's joy shine forth, poor dear!
Were she and I alone, then would you see it!"[3]
And Pagamin replies: "Well then, so be it.
Go, take her to her chamber, sire." And so,
Indeed, he did, closing the door thereof
And speaking thus: "Bartholomée, my love!
Pray, look upon my face. What? Do you know
Me not? Your Quinzica? Your husband, who
Has never faltered in his love for you!
Am I so changed? So altered? If I am,
Clear is the cause therefor: my fear, madame,
Of what your privateering rogue might do;
My sadness at your loss. Tell me, did ever
I fail to grant your slightest wish whatever?
Clothes, pleasures... Was I not your very slave?
And slave, madame, is what you too shall be
If you remain the captive of this knave.
Think of your honor!" "Honor?" she retorted,
Breaking her silence, finally. "Honor? Tell me,
Where was my honor when I was consorted
With such as you, monsieur? Did they not sell me,
Young and unwilling, fresh and flushed with life,
To languish, wasted, as an old man's wife?
Worthy was I of better than befell me!
Gladly would I have known the joys and bliss
Of marriage, ready as I was to do them
Homage and justice. But I never knew them—
Nay, not a whit! Now has it come to this.
Your holy days! Oh, how I came to rue them,
Monsieur! Day in day out, the same old song!

Mais Pagamin, si-tost qu'il m'eut ravie,
Me sceut donner bien une autre leçon.
J'ay plus appris des choses de la vie
Depuis deux jours, qu'en quatre ans avec vous.
Laissez-moi donc, Monsieur mon cher Epoux.
Sur mon retour n'insistez davantage.
Calendriers ne sont point en usage
Chez Pagamin: je vous en avertis.
Vous et les miens avez merité pis.
Vous pour avoir mal mesuré vos forces
En m'épousant; eux pour s'estre mépris
En preferant les legeres amorces
De quelque bien à cet autre point-là.
Mais Pagamin pour tous y pourvoira.
Il ne sçait Loy, ny Digeste, ny Code;
Et cependant tres-bonne est sa methode.
De ce matin luy-mesme il vous dira
Du quart en sus comme la chose en va.
Un tel aveu vous surprend et vous touche:
Mais faire icy de la petite bouche
Ne sert de rien; l'on n'en croira pas moins.
Et puis qu'enfin nous voicy sans témoins:
Adieu vous dis, vous, et vos jours de Feste.
Je suis de chair, les habits rien n'y font:
Vous sçavez bien, Monsieur, qu'entre la teste
Et le talon d'autres affaires sont.
A tant se teut. Richard tombé des nuës,
Fut tout heureux de pouvoir s'en aller.
Bartholomée ayant ses hontes beuës
Ne se fit pas tenir pour demeurer.
Le pauvre Epoux en eut tant de tristesse,

But Pagamin sings different tunes, and taught me
More in two days—since first he seized (not bought!) me—
Than ever you could do these four years long.
So go your way and leave me, husband dear.
Never shall I return to you. For here
We have no calendars, nor need we such.
Your chastisement is surely not as much
As you deserve: you, and my parents too.
You, sire, for biting more than you could chew
In wedding me; and they, for caring not
What I would get, but only what they got.
Well, Pagamin makes up for all of you.
True, laws and codes and all are not his forte.
Yet is his method sound. When he pays court
He pays with interest! And this morning shall he
Give you a good account and proper tally.
My frankness shocks and startles you, no doubt,
Monsieur. But it will do no good to pout
And hang about, and longer dillydally.
Be off and go your way. For, *entre nous*,
I have for you but one word more: Adieu!
You and your saints' days, feasts, fasts, masses all!
Clothes and the like are fine. But please recall,
A wife is made of flesh, and has a deal
Of more important things 'twixt head and heel."
And that was that. The judge, at her behest,
Appalled, but glad to save his neck, withdraws.
Shame to the winds, Madame—no hems, no haws—
Remains, content to be the corsair's guest.
Wherewith her spouse, poor soul, grows so distressed—
Oppressed by ills of age as well—that he

Outre les maux qui suivent la vieillesse,

Qu'il en mourut à quelques jours de là;
Et Pagamin prit à femme sa Veuve.
Ce fut bien fait: nul des deux ne tomba
Dans l'accident du pauvre Quinzica,
S'estans choisis l'un et l'autre à l'épreuve.
Belle leçon pour gens à cheveux gris;
Sinon qu'ils soient d'humeur accommodante:
Car en ce cas Messieurs les favoris
Font leur ouvrage, et la Dame est contente.

Proceeds to die. The pirate thereupon
Weds his Bartholomée; and they live on
Untouched by any such catastrophe
As erstwhile husband Quinzica had known;
For theirs the choice—well tried!—and theirs alone.
Greybeards take heed! They who would buy a bride
Can learn from this; save those who, blinking-eyed,
Look on as wives do what they please, disporting
Under their nose, with beaus and swains cavorting.
Happy such wives as these, well satisfied!

The Greybeards' Calendar

A femme avare galant escroc

Nouvelle tirée de Bocace

Qu'un homme soit plumé par des Coquetes,
Ce n'est pour faire au miracle crier.
Gratis est mort: plus d'Amour sans payer:
En beaux Louys se content les fleuretes.
Ce que je dis des Coquetes s'entend.
Pour nostre honneur sì me faut-il pourtant
Monstrer qu'on peut nonobstant leur adresse
En attraper au moins une entre cent;
Et luy joüer quelque jour de soûplesse.
Je choisiray pour exemple Gulphar.
Le Drosle fit un trait de franc Soudar;
Car aux faveurs d'une Belle il eut part
Sans débourser, escroquant la Chrestienne.
Notez cecy, et qu'il vous en souvienne
Galants d'épée; encor bien que ce tour
Pour vous styler soit fort peu necessaire;
Je trouverois maintenant à la Cour
Plus d'un Gulphar si j'en avois affaire.
Celuy-cy donc chez sire Gasparin
Tant frequenta, qu'il devint à la fin
De son Epouse amoureux sans mesure.
Elle estoit jeune, et belle creature,
Plaisoit beaucoup, fors un poinct qui gastoit
Toute l'affaire, et qui seul rebutoit
Les plus ardens; c'est qu'elle estoit avare.
Ce n'est pas chose en ce siecle fort rare.
Je l'ay jà dit, rien n'y font les soûpirs.
Celuy-là parle une langue Barbare
Qui l'or en main n'explique ses desirs.

The Greedy Woman Gallantly Deceived

How changed is love, today, from days of old!
Coquettes abound, eager to fleece their prey.
Sweet nothings echo with the ring of gold:
"Gratis" is dead; those who would love must pay.
Such are, I fear, the ways of our coquettes.
But, for man's honor, needs must I confess
That, still, one in a hundred of them gets
Herself caught up, despite her artfulness,
Victim of man's deceptions nonetheless.
A case in point: There was a knavish gent—
Gulphar by name—who, to his heart's content,
Did dalliance with a certain fine beldame,
And yet it cost him not one single cent.
Pay heed, swashbuckling braves. Learn how this came
To pass; although your own sly tricks are such,
That his, indeed, will hardly teach you much:
The court has more than one Gulphar, I vow!
This one—the subject of my tale—frequented
His friend, one Gasparin, quite often. Now,
So often, that he could not be prevented,
In time, from coveting the latter's wife,
Grown soon the love—nay, passion!—of his life:
Young, fair, and winsome, save for one defect;
One of those irksome, all-consuming flaws,
That gave the lady's would-be gallants pause—
And cause, in fact, to be more circumspect:
To wit, her greedy, avaricious bent.
Not rare in times like ours, when, in effect,
A lover's languid sighs are breath ill-spent;

Le jeu, la jupe, et l'Amour des plaisirs,
Sont les ressorts que Cupidon employe:
De leur boutique il sort chez les François
Plus de Cocus que du cheval de Troye
Il ne sortit de Heros autresfois.
Pour revenir à l'humeur de la Belle,
Le compagnon ne pût rien tirer d'elle
Qu'il ne parlast. Chacun sçait ce que c'est
Que de parler: le Lecteur s'il luy plaist,
Me permettra de dire ainsi la chose.
Gulphar donc parle, et si bien qu'il propose
Deux cens écus. La Belle l'écouta:
Et Gasparin à Gulphar les presta
(Ce fut le bon), puis aux champs s'en alla,
Ne soupçonnant aucunement sa femme.
Gulphar les donne en presence de gens.
Voila, dit-il, deux cens écus contans,
Qu'à vostre Epoux vous donnerez, Madame.
La Belle crut qu'il avoit dit cela
Par politique, et pour joüer son rôle.
Le lendemain elle le regala
Tout de son mieux, en femme de parole.
Le Drosle en prit ce jour et les suivans
Pour son argent, et mesme avec usure:
A bon payeur on fait bonne mesure.
Quand Gasparin fut de retour des champs,
Gulphar luy dit, son Epouse presente:
J'ay vostre argent à Madame rendu,
N'en ayant eu pour une affaire urgente

Meaningless tongue: vain babble voiced for nought.
For money it is that talks; love must be bought.
Gaming, philandering, gay merriment—
Such are the strings to Cupid's bow. With these
He makes more cuckolds of our French, perforce,
Than there poured heroes from that Trojan Horse!...
Most ardent of milady's devotees,
Gulphar would surely meet with no success—
No favors would he have of her—unless
He deigned to speak her language. (May it please
The reader: he knows well enough, I guess,
What "speak her language" means!) And so, indeed,
He spoke: "Two hundred crowns..." She listened well.
What's more, her husband Gasparin agreed
To lend the sum—fine ninny, truth to tell!
After which he went off, leaving the belle,
With never a fear for her fidelity.
Gulphar arrives; and, others standing near,
Gives her the money, for the rest to see,
Saying: "Madame, please pay this debt for me:
Two hundred crowns I owe our good *messire*."
Admiring his finesse, she thinks him quite
The clever actor. Whereupon, next night,
As promised, she gives what he paid her for.
And several nights thereafter. *Et encore...*
He takes it gladly, much to his delight,
Getting his money's worth, and then much more.
Soon Gasparin returns. Gulphar comes by,
And says: "My friend, your loan... I found I had

Aucun besoin, comme je l'avois crû:
Déchargez en vostre livre de grace.
A ce propos aussi froide que glace
Nostre Galande avoüa le receu.
Qu'eust-elle fait? on eust prouvé la chose.
Son regret fut d'avoir enflé la doze
De ses faveurs; c'est ce qui la fâchoit:
Voyez un peu la perte que c'estoit!
En la quittant Gulphar alla tout droit
Conter ce cas, le corner par la Ville,
Le publier, le prescher sur les toits.
De l'en blâmer, il seroit inutile:
Ainsi vit on chez nous autres François.

No need of it, in fact. Next day I bade
Your wife, here present—she will verify—
To take it back. Pray clear me of my debt."
With icy stare, the now-outdone coquette,
Glaring in disbelief, nodded, agreeing.
What else? The proof had been there for the seeing.
What vexed her most, her most extreme regret,
Was her excessive dose of boon bestowed.
Gulphar strode off, proud of his artifice.
Eager to tell his friends, he promptly crowed
His triumph from the roofs. Why not? In this,
He only did what, in such circumstance,
Most any man would do today in France.

On ne s'avise jamais de tout

Conte tiré des Cent Nouvelles Nouvelles

Certain jaloux ne dormant que d'un œil,
Interdisoit tout commerce à sa femme.
Dans le dessein de prévenir la Dame,
Il avoit fait un fort ample recueil
De tous les tours que le sexe sçait faire.
Pauvre ignorant! comme si cette affaire
N'estoit une hydre, à parler franchement.
Il captivoit sa femme cependant;
De ses cheveux vouloit sçavoir le nombre;
La faisoit suivre, à toute heure, en tous lieux,
Par une vieille au corps tout remply d'yeux,
Qui la quittoit aussi peu que son ombre.
Ce fou tenoit son recueil fort entier:
Il le portoit en guise de Psautier,
Croyant par là cocuage hors de game.
Un jour de feste, arrive que la Dame
En revenant de l'Eglise passa
Prés d'un logis, d'où quelqu'un luy jetta
Fort à propos plein un pannier d'ordure.
On s'excusa: la pauvre creature
Toute vilaine entra dans le logis.
Il luy falut dépoüiller ses habits.
Elle envoya querir une autre jupe,
Dés en entrant, par cette doüagna,
Qui hors d'haleine à Monsieur raconta
Tout l'accident. Foin, dit-il, celuy-là
N'est dans mon Livre, et je suis pris pour dupe:
Que le recueil au diable soit donné.
Il disoit bien; car on n'avoit jetté

The Best-Laid Plans

A certain jealous husband never slept.
So greatly feared he lest his wife abuse
His trust, that, in most apt detail he kept
A list of every clever hoax and ruse
That creatures of her sex adeptly use.
The simple soul! As if their fraud were less
Than hydra-headed, frankly speaking. Yet
He fairly held her captive, in duress;
Counted her every hair; and never let
Her leave, without a myriad-eyeballed crone
Following after, as a chaperone,
Tight as her very shadow, if not tighter.
Our poor, benighted husband, ever wary
Of wife's design, was certain that, despite her,
Thanks to his list—like holy breviary—
He would keep dreaded cuckoldry at bay.
Now then, it happened that, one holiday,
Coming from church, said crone-escorted spouse,
Beneath a window, hears the "gardyloo!"
As someone, suddenly, from in the house,
Souses her with his slops. What can she do?
Apologies... Excuses... In she goes,
Promptly throws off her swill-bespattered clothes,
And sends the duenna running home to fetch
Another skirt; whose breathless "ahs" and "ohs"
Inform the husband of the deed. "The wretch,"
He cries. "Damnation! That's one trick I missed!
I've been deceived! The Devil take my list!"
And he was right. It was no accident.

Cette immondice, et la Dasme gasté,
Qu'afin qu'elle eust quelque valable excuse
Pour éloigner son dragon quelque-temps.
Un sien Galant amy de là dedans
Tout aussi-tost profita de la ruse.
Nous avons beau sur ce sexe avoir l'œil:
Ce n'est coup seur encontre tous esclandres.
Maris jaloux, brûlez vostre Recueil
Sur ma parole, et faites-en des cendres.

Those slops were heaved, in truth, with one intent:
To rid the lady of her dragoness—
A little while at least—thereby providing
Her cunning suitor, in the house residing,
Much profit from the state of her undress.
So, jealous husbands, waste not your attention
On sex whose wit appalls and wile abashes.
Against their bag of tricks there's no prevention.
As for your lists... Best burn them all to ashes.

Le Villageois qui cherche son veau

Conte tiré des Cent Nouvelles Nouvelles

Un Villageois ayant perdu son Veau,
L'alla chercher dans la forest prochaine.
Il se plaça sur l'arbre le plus beau,
Pour mieux entendre, et pour voir dans la plaine.
Vient une Dame avec un jouvenceau.
Le lieu leur plaist, l'eau leur vient à la bouche:
Et le Galant, qui sur l'herbe la couche,
Crie en voyant je ne sçay quels appas:
O Dieux, que vois-je, et que ne vois-je pas!
Sans dire quoy; car c'estoient lettres closes.
Lors le Manant les arrestant tout coy:
Homme de bien, qui voyez tant de choses,
Voyez-vous point mon Veau? dites-le moy.

The Peasant Who Goes Looking for His Calf

A peasant lost his calf, and thought
That in the wood it could be found;
So climbed a tree wherefrom he sought
To see and hear, the forest round.
A lad appearing with his lass—
Who find the place a savory spot—
Laying the maiden on the grass,
Shouts as he spies I know not what:
"Ye gods! Such things! What things I see!
And what not!" (He declines to tell.)
Peasant cuts short their *vis-à-vis*:
"Good sir, who see so much, maybe,
I pray, you see my calf as well?"

L'Anneau d'Hans Carvel

Conte tiré de R. [1]

Hans Carvel prit sur ses vieux ans
Femme jeune en toute maniere;
Il prit aussi soucis cuisans;
Car l'un sans l'autre ne va guere.
Babeau (c'est la jeune Femelle,
Fille du Bailly Concordat)
Fut du bon poil, ardente, et belle,
Et propre à l'amoureux combat.
Carvel craignant de sa nature
Le cocuage et les railleurs,
Alleguoit à la creature,
Et la legende, et l'écriture,
Et tous les Livres les meilleurs:
Blâmoit les visites secretes;
Frondoit l'attirail des Coquetes;
Et contre un monde de recettes,
Et de moyens de plaire aux yeux,
Invectivoit tout de son mieux.
A tous ces discours la Galande
Ne s'arrestoit aucunement;
Et de Sermons n'estoit friande
A moins qu'ils fussent d'un Amant.
Cela faisoit que le bon sire
Ne sçavoit tantost plus qu'y dire;
Eust voulu souvent estre mort.
Il eut pourtant dans son martyre
Quelques momens de reconfort:
L'histoire en est tres-veritable.
Une nuit, qu'ayant tenu table,

Hans Carvel's Ring

Hans Carvel married, late in life,
A maid of tender years. But oh!
What bale she caused him, and what woe!
For so, forsooth, it goes. His wife,
The bailiff's daughter—one Babeau,
Née Concordat—was passing fair,
Passionate, sprightly, debonair;
Well fit for love's encounters, quite.
Fearing the horns of cuckoldry
And ridicule, our neophyte
Would ever quote and ever cite
From every known authority—
And Holy Writ—counseling her
To be on guard lest sly monsieur
Come wooing, in shameful secrecy;
Lest she, to her (and his!) regret,
Mimic the wiles of vain coquette
To please man's eye. How he would rail,
And rave, and rant... To no avail.
Sermons and speeches: useless chatter—
Save those her suitors uttered at her!
Thus did the good Hans Carvel fail
Of his intent; indeed, the matter
So sore distressed him that, instead,
He wished he might betimes be dead.
Yet, in his martyrdom, did he
Know moments of relief. This story
Is true, I vouch and guarantee.
One night (when he has, a priori,

Et bû force bon vin nouveau,
Carvel ronfloit prés de Babeau,
Il luy fut avis que le diable
Luy mettoit au doigt un anneau;
Qu'il luy disoit: Je sçais la peine
Qui te tourmente, et qui te gesne;
Carvel, j'ay pitié de ton cas;
Tien cette bague, et ne la lâches.
Car tandis qu'au doigt tu l'auras,
Ce que tu crains point ne seras,
Point ne seras sans que le sçaches.
—Trop ne puis vous remercier,
Dit Carvel, la faveur est grande.
Monsieur Satan, Dieu vous le rende,
Grandmercy Monsieur l'Aumônier.
Là dessus achevant son somme,
Et les yeux encore aggravez,
Il se trouva que le bon homme
Avoit le doigt où vous sçavez.

Eaten and drunk—long, leisurely—
Fine food, new wine), snoring abed
Beside Babeau, he dreams Old Ned—
The Devil—come a-visiting,
Onto his finger slips a ring,
Telling him: "Hans, I know your strife,
Your torment, fear, woe—everything.
But if you wear this ring, your wife
Will ever faithful be, I swear;
And never shall you grow—no, never!—
Those horns that you so fear to wear,
But free shall be of them forever."
"Satan," cries Hans, "may God repay
Your service done to me this day!
I thank you, sire, for your largesse,
Your kindness, and your thoughtfulness."
Then he awakes, about to rise.
But when he goes to rub his eyes,
Where is his finger? You can guess.

Hans Carvel's Ring

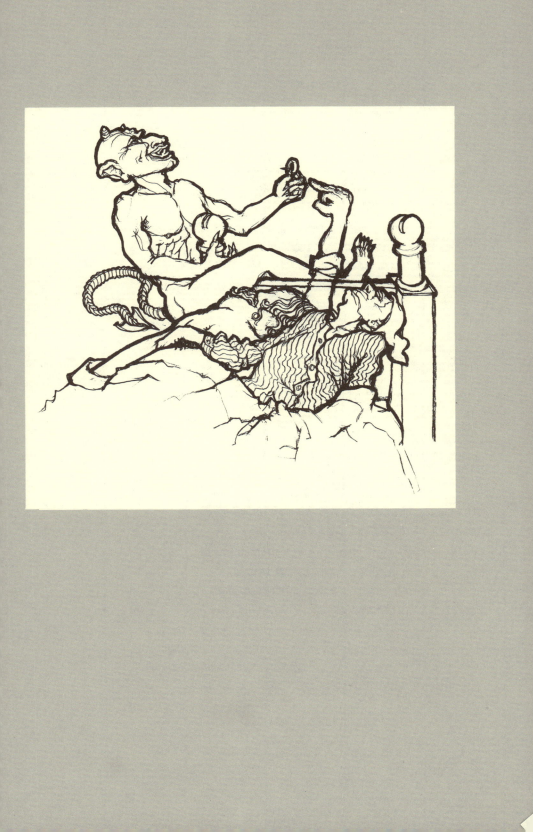

Le Gascon puny

Nouvelle

    Un Gascon, pour s'estre vanté
    De posseder certaine Belle,
    Fut puny de sa vanité
    D'une façon assez nouvelle.
Il se vantoit à faux, et ne possedoit rien.
Mais quoy! tout médisant est Prophete en ce monde:
On croit le mal d'abord; mais à l'égard du bien,
    Il faut qu'un public en réponde.
La Dame cependant du Gascon se moquoit:
Même au logis pour luy rarement elle estoit:
    Et bien souvent qu'il la traitoit
    D'incomparable, et de divine,
    La Belle aussi-tost s'enfuyoit,
    S'allant sauver chez sa voisine.
Elle avoit nom Philis, son voisin Eurilas,
La voisine Cloris, le Gascon Dorilas,
Un sien amy Damon: c'est tout, si j'ay memoire.
Ce Damon, de Cloris, à ce que dit l'histoire,
Estoit Amant aymé, Galant, comme on voudra,
Quelque chose de plus encor que tout cela.
Pour Philis, son humeur libre, gaye, et sincere
    Monstroit qu'elle estoit sans affaire,
    Sans secret, et sans passion.
On ignoroit le prix de sa possession:
Seulement à l'user chacun la croyoit bonne.
Elle approchoit vingt-ans; et venoit d'enterrer
Un mary (de ceux-là que l'on perd sans pleurer,
Vieux barbon qui laissoit d'écus plein une tonne).
    En mille endroits de sa personne

The Gascon's Punishment

A braggart Gascon, having said
That he had brought a certain belle to bed,
   Was punished for his boastful lies
   In new and most uncommon wise.[1]
For no one had he bedded; none at all.
(But lying knaves are prophets here below:
Gladly we lend our ear to ill; although
   When one says good, we need, withal,
Witnesses by the score before we heed it.)
Though fairer than the goddesses he found her,
Philis—the lady—scorned our Gascon bounder;
   And every time he called, indeed, it
Pleased her to go seek refuge with her friend,
Cloris. Wherefore, much though he might intend
To plead his passion, never could he plead it.
   The Gascon's name is Dorilas.
   As for the rest, the list is small:
Cloris is married to one Eurilas,
But spends her time in amorous folderol—
Or call it what you will—with tender beau:
   Damon, by name. (As I recall,
Those are the only names you need to know.)
Philis, the belle, was footloose, fancy-free:
No swain, no secret paramour had she.
   Men found her fit for bed; but oh!
Though bed the lass they would—and none would doubt it—
   No one knew how to go about it.
Not yet full twenty years, yet had she just
   Buried a husband, passing old

La Belle avoit dequoy mettre un Gascon aux Cieux,
    Des attraits par-dessus les yeux,
    Je ne sçay quel air de pucelle,
    Mais le cœur tant soit peu rebelle;
Rebelle toutesfois de la bonne façon.
    Voila Philis. Quant au Gascon,
    Il estoit Gascon, c'est tout dire.
    Je laisse à penser si le sire
Importuna la Veuve, et s'il fit des sermens.
    Ceux des Gascons et des Normans
    Passent peu pour mots d'Evangile.
    C'estoit pourtant chose facile
De croire Dorilas de Philis amoureux;
Mais il vouloit aussi que l'on le crust heureux.
Philis dissimulant, dit un jour à cet homme:
    Je veux un service de vous:
    Ce n'est pas d'aller jusqu'à Rome;
C'est que vous nous aydiez à tromper un jaloux.
La chose est sans peril, et mesme fort aisée.
    Nous voulons que cette nuit-cy
    Vous couchiez avec le mary
    De Cloris, qui m'en a priée.
    Avec Damon s'estant broüillée,
Il leur faut une nuit entiere, et par delà,
Pour démêler entre-eux tout ce differend-là.
    Nostre but est qu'Eurilas pense,
Vous sentant prés de luy, que ce soit sa moitié.
Il ne luy touche point, vit dedans l'abstinence,
Et soit par jalousie, ou bien par impuissance,
A retranché d'Hymen certains droits d'amitié;
    Ronfle toûjours, fait la nuit d'une traite:

(One of those fusty greybeards young wives must
Not weep to lose), who left a ton of gold.
A thousand things about her person might
Give any proper Gascon much delight.
A bodyful of charms; a virgin air;
   A heart a trifle willful, yet,
   For all that, no less debonair:
Such were the qualities of our coquette.
   As for our Gascon friend... Just let
Me say he was a Gascon: that should tell you.
   And did he importune her? Well, you
   Surely might say so! Constantly!
With plight and pledge. (But those of Gascony—
Normandy too—make promises galore:
The Gospel ought they not be taken for!)
At any rate, it was not hard to see
How much the vain pretender loved. What's more,
   He wanted all to think that he
Had met with great success. Now she, one day,
Dissembling, came and told him: "Sire, I pray
You render me a service. Aye, a boon.
   Nay, not to travel to the moon;
Merely to help deceive, in fitting wise,
Cloris's jealous husband. Thus, my friend,
   Much will you please me if you spend
   The night, abed, in her disguise.
   Damon and she need time to mend
A lover's quarrel: one night, end to end.
   Eurilas, lying thus beside you,
Will take you for his wife. But have no fear.
   No harm, I promise, can betide you:

C'est assez qu'en son lit il trouve une cornette.
Nous vous ajusterons: enfin, ne craignez rien:
    Je vous recompenseray bien.
Pour se rendre Philis un peu plus favorable,
Le Gascon eust couché, dit il, avec le diable.
La nuit vient, on le coëfe, on le met au grand lit,
On esteint les flambeaux, Eurilas prend sa place;
    Du Gascon le peur se saisit;
    Il devient aussi froid que glace;
    N'oseroit tousser ny cracher,
    Beaucoup moins encor' s'approcher:
Se fait petit, se serre, au bord se va nicher,
Et ne tient que moitié de la rive occupée:
Je crois qu'on l'auroit mis dans un fourreau d'épée.
Son coucheur cette nuit se retourna cent fois;
Et jusques sur le nez luy porta certains doigts
    Que la peur luy fit trouver rudes.
    Le pis de ses inquietudes,
C'est qu'il craignoit qu'enfin un caprice amoureux
Ne prist à ce mary: tels cas sont dangereux,
Lors que l'un des conjoints se sent privé du somme.
Toûjours nouveaux sujets alarmoient le pauvre homme.
L'on étendoit un pied; l'on approchoit un bras:
Il crût mesme sentir la barbe d'Eurilas.
Mais voicy quelque chose à mon sens de terrible.
Une sonnette estoit prés du chevet du lit:
Eurilas de sonner, et faire un bruit horrible.
    Le Gascon se pâme à ce bruit;
    Cette fois-là se croit détruit;
    Fait un vœu, renonce à sa Dame;
    Et songe au salut de son ame.

Abstinent is our jealous cavalier—
Or impotent, perchance. Nought does he now—
Chastely neglectful of the marriage vow—
Save snore the whole night through. Let him but find
A figure, nightcapped in the female style,
    Sharing his bed—all cowled the while—
    And will he lie content. Now, mind,
Do me this service and, if done aright,
You shall be recompensed." The Gascon said,
To win her favor he would go to bed
With Lucifer himself. And so that night—
Coifed, veiled—they tuck him in, blow out the light...
    Come Eurilas, to rest his head,
    And soon our Gascon, chilled with fright—
Cornered, afraid to move, to cough, to spit—
    Cringes and huddles, grown so small
    And slim, I venture he could fit
    Into a scabbard, cowl and all.
Alas, his bedmate tossed and turned so much
    That, with his fingers, rude of touch,
He fairly picked the Gascon's nose. And yet,
    The thought that most tormented him
    Was that monsieur might, on a whim,
Be moved—here, now!—to have an *amourette*.
Danger indeed! And thus, 'midst probing limb
(And face so close he thinks that he can smell
The goodman's beard!), the sleepless night wears on...
When Eurilas, awaking, rings his bell,
The noise, good God, is such that, thereupon
    The Gascon, swooning and undone,
Swears to renounce the lady; and—half dead

Personne ne venant, Eurilas s'endormit.
            Avant qu'il fust jour on ouvrit.
Philis l'avoit promis; quand voicy de plus belle
            Un flambeau comble de tous maux.
            Le Gascon aprés ces travaux
            Se fust bien levé sans chandelle.
Sa perte estoit alors un poinct tout asseuré.
On approche du lit. Le pauvre homme éclairé
            Prie Eurilas qu'il luy pardonne.
            Je le veux, dit une personne
            D'un ton de voix remply d'appas.
            C'estoit Philis, qui d'Eurilas
Avoit tenu la place, et qui sans trop attendre
            Tout en chemise s'alla rendre
Dans les bras de Cloris qu'accompagnoit Damon.
C'estoit, dis-je, Philis, qui conta du Gascon
            La peine et la frayeur extrême;
Et qui pour l'obliger à se tuer soy-mesme,
        En luy montrant ce qu'il avoit perdu,
            Laissoit son sein à demy nu.

From fear—to save his soul instead.
But no one comes. No, not a one.
And Eurilas falls back to sleep again...
Time passes (none too swiftly!)... Then,
Still before dawn, the door swings wide:
As promised! And his saviors step inside—
Or so he thinks! For, woe of woes, they bring
A torch, that lights room, bed, him... Everything!
Better the dark!... But no! Now, terrified,
He begs the husband's pardon. "Yes,"
Replies a voice a-lilt with winsomeness:
Philis's voice! For she it was who had
Contrived, in Eurilas's stead,
To teach a lesson to the lying cad;
She who, in nightshirt, bounding from the bed,
Hugging Cloris, and laughing, out of breath—
Damon as well—recounts her Gascon's fear and dread;
And who, to make him hate himself to death,
And show him what he missed, has now disclosed
Her comely bosom, half exposed.

L'Hermite

Nouvelle tirée de Bocace

    Dame Venus, et Dame Hypocrisie,
Font quelquefois ensemble de bons coups;
Tout homme est homme, les Hermites sur tous;
Ce que j'en dis ce n'est point par envie.
Avez-vous Sœur, Fille, ou Femme jolie,
Gardez le froc; c'est un maistre Gonin;
Vous en tenez s'il tombe sous sa main
Belle qui soit quelque peu simple et neuve:
Pour vous montrer que je ne parle en vain,
Lisez cecy, je ne veux autre preuve.

    Un jeune Hermite estoit tenu pour Saint:
On luy gardoit place dans la Legende.
L'homme de Dieu d'une corde estoit ceint
Pleine de nœuds; mais sous sa houpelande
Logeoit le cœur d'un dangereux paillard.
Un Chapelet pendoit à sa ceinture
Long d'une brasse, et gros outre mesure;
Une clochette estoit de l'autre part.
Au demeurant, il faisoit le caphard,
Se renfermoit voyant une femelle
Dedans sa coque, et baissoit la prunelle:
Vous n'auriez dit qu'il eust mangé le lard.

    Un bourg estoit dedans son voisinage,
Et dans ce Bourg une Veuve fort sage,
Qui demeuroit tout à l'extremité.
Elle n'avoit pour tout bien qu'une fille,
Jeune, ingenuë, agreable et gentille;
Pucelle encor; mais à la verité
Moins par vertu que par simplicité;

The Hermit

Venus and Dame Hypocrisy, abreast,
Often commit their infamy together.
Now, men are human; and it's doubtful whether
Hermits or monks are holier than the rest.[1]
Nor is it envy, as one might suggest,
That makes me thus observe. Have you a wife,
A sister, or perchance a daughter fair?
Beware, monsieur! Best guard her with your life
Against the cloth. For, devious they who wear
Those robes.[2] And any beauty just a bit
Naïve in love, or somewhat weak of wit,
Will give you cause to fret, caught in their snare.
Read on. My tale gives ample proof of it.
  A hermit once there was, of tender age;
And yet so holy that he had a page
Reserved already in the saintly writ.
Girt with a many-knotted cord, God's sage
And pious-appearing hermit, all the same,
Harbored a heart steeped deep in lust and shame.
A chaplet—fathom-long, uncommon size—
Hung from his belt; a bell as well. And should
A female creature chance his way, he would—
Foul humbug!—scurry off with downcast eyes.
No fast-day glut-lard he! Nay! Heaven forfend!...
  Now, near where dwelt our oh-so-righteous friend
There stood a town; and there, in humblest wise,
A widow lived, out at the farthest end.
A daughter was, I fear, the only prize
That she possessed: young, artless, fair, untouched...
But if her virgin flower lay yet unsmutched,

Peu d'entregent, beaucoup d'honnesteté,
D'autre dot point, d'Amans pas davantage.
Du temps d'Adam qu'on naissoit tout vestu,
Je pense bien que la Belle en eût eu,
Car avec rien on montoit un mesnage.
Il ne faloit matelas ny linçeul:
Mesme le lit n'estoit pas necessaire.
Ce temps n'est plus. Himen qui marchoit seul,
Meine à present à sa suite un Notaire.
    L'Anachorete, en questant par le Bourg,
Vid cette fille, et dit sous son capuce:
Voicy dequoy; si tu sçais quelque tour,
Il te le faut employer, Frere Luce.
Pas n'y manqua, voicy comme il s'y prit.
Elle logeoit, comme j'ay déja dit,
Tout prés des champs, dans une maisonnette,
Dont la cloison par nostre Anachorete
Estant percée aisément et sans bruit,
Le Compagnon par une belle nuit,
(Belle, non pas, le vent et la tempeste
Favorisoient le dessein du Galant)
Une nuit donc, dans le pertuis mettant
Un long cornet, tout du haut de la teste
Il leur cria: Femmes escoutez-moy.
A cette voix, toutes pleines d'effroy,
Se blotissant, l'une et l'autre est en trance.
Il continuë, et corne à toute outrance:
Réveillez-vous Creatures de Dieu,
Toy femme Veuve, et toy fille pucelle:
Allez trouver mon serviteur fidelle
L'Hermite Luce, et partez de ce lieu

Virtue was less to blame than simpleness:
Good character, but not much politesse.
As for her dowry, sadly, even less!³
And beaux? No, none. What would they do with her?
(In Adam's time, when we wore birthday suits
And slept—unmattressed and unsheeted brutes—
Au naturel, the belle, unless I err,
Would have been wooed by more than one monsieur.
Then Marriage walked alone. Now, *au contraire*,
Notaries dog his footsteps everywhere...)
   Well, one fine day it finally comes to pass:
The monk, with sanctimonious gait—up, down,
Begging for alms round and about the town—
At length espies the comely, sprightly lass
And whispers to himself beneath his cloak:
"Frère Luce, if you have wiles prepare to use them!"
He had; he did; as these poor gentlefolk
Soon came to learn. Here's how he would abuse them:
Mother and daughter dwelt, as I have said,
By village edge; modest, at most, their shed.
The wall was thin: it took him but a minute,
No more, to pierce a hole discreetly in it.
Then, one fine night... In fact, not really fine:
A storm, in truth, abetted his design...
At any rate, as I was saying, one night,
Through it he placed a horn, about ear height,
Into it shouting: "Women! Hear me, pray!"
They, at the voice, were filled with such dismay,
Such fear—nay, utter awe!—that, in their fright,
Spellbound, they huddled, as again he roared:
"Awake! Awake, ye servants of the Lord!

Demain matin sans le dire à personne;
Car c'est ainsi que le Ciel vous l'ordonne.
Ne craignez point, je conduiray vos pas,
Luce est benin. Toy Veuve tu feras
Que de ta fille il ait la compagnie;
Car d'eux doit naistre un Pape, dont la vie
Reformera tout le peuple Chrestien.
La chose fut tellement prononcée,
Que dans le lit l'une et l'autre enfoncée,
Ne laissa pas de l'entendre fort bien.
La peur les tint un quart-d'heure en silence.
La fille enfin met le nez hors des draps,
Et puis tirant sa Mere par le bras,
Luy dit d'un ton tout remply d'innocence:
Mon Dieu, Maman, y faudra-t-il aller?
Ma compagnie? helas! qu'en veut-il faire?
Je ne sçay pas comment il faut parler;
Ma cousine Anne est bien mieux son affaire
Et retiendroit bien mieux tous ses Sermons.
—Sotte, tay toy, luy repartit la Mere,
C'est bien celà; va, va, pour ces leçons
Il n'est besoin de tout l'esprit du monde:
Dés la première, ou bien dés la seconde,
Ta cousine Anne en sçaura moins que toy.
—Oüy? dit la fille, hé mon Dieu, menez-moy.
Partons, bien-tost nous reviendrons au giste.
—Tout doux, reprit la Mere en soûriant,
Il ne faut pas que nous allions si viste:
Car que sçait-on? le diable est bien meschant,
Et bien trompeur; si c'estoit luy ma fille
Qui fust venu pour nous tendre des lacs?

Thou, widow. And thou, daughter undefiled!
Go ye at dawn, in silence, from this spot,
And find my faithful minion, Luce the mild.
Such is the will of heaven, so fail ye not!
Nor need ye fear, for I shall lead ye to him.
Once there, thou, widow, thou must do thy best
To see that she, thy virgin daughter, shew him
Courtesy and attention. For, much blessed
Will be their union. From it shall there spring
A pope! A pope, whose holy life shall bring
Great comfort to the whole of Christendom!"
So clear the message was that—overcome,
And numb with fright—though burrowed deep abed,
They heard each word aright. Much time went by.
At last the daughter, timid, poked her head,
Tugged at her mother's arm, and, guileless, said:
"My God, mama! Must we go, you and I?
My courtesy and my attention? Why,
Whatever would he want with them, I wonder?
Besides, I know I'm bound to make some blunder.
My cousin Anne, I vow, would be much better.
More courteous and attentive... Shall I get her?
She'll learn his lessons, whereas I..." "By thunder!"
Her mother interrupts. "Don't be an ass!
For lessons like the ones he's going to show you,
You needn't be the cunningest in class.
After he gives you one or two, I know you
Surely will know far more than Anne; although you
Know next to nothing now—or less, alas!"
"Oh? Well, for goodness' sake then... Yes, let's go."
"Not quite so fast!" replies the widow, smiling.

As tu pris garde? il parloit d'un ton cas,
Comme je croy que parle la famille
De Lucifer. Le fait merite bien
Que sans courir ny precipiter rien,
Nous nous gardions de nous laisser surprendre.
Si la frayeur t'avoit fait mal entendre:
Pour moy j'avois l'esprit tout éperdu.
—Non, non, Maman, j'ay fort bien entendu,
Dit la fillette.—Or bien reprit la Mere,
Puis qu'ainsi va, mettons-nous en priere.
   Le lendemain, tout le jour se passa
A raisonner, et par cy, et par là,
Sur cette voix et sur cette rencontre.
La nuit venuë arrive le corneur:
Il leur cria d'un ton à faire peur:
Femme incredule et qui vas alencontre
Des volontez de Dieu ton Createur,
Ne tarde plus, va t'en trouver l'Hermite,
Ou tu mourras. La fillette reprit:
Hé bien, Maman, l'avois-je pas bien dit?
Mon Dieu partons; allons rendre visite
A l'Homme saint; je crains tant vostre mort
Que j'y courrois, et tout de mon plus fort,
S'il le faloit.—Allons donc, dit la Mere.
La Belle mit son corset des bons jours,
Son demy-ceint, ses pendans de velours,
Sans se douter de ce qu'elle alloit faire:
Jeune fillette a toûjours soin de plaire.
Nostre Cagot s'estoit mis aux aguets,
Et par un trou qu'il avoit fait exprés
A sa Cellule, il vouloit que ces femmes

"Clever the Devil's wiles, ever beguiling.
Best we go slowly child, lest, to our woe,
We fall into a trap. That voice—harsh, hoarse—
Sounded like Lucifer, or one of his.
For now, I think the wisest counsel is,
Surely, to wait and let time run its course.
So frightened were we that we scarcely heard..."
"Oh no, mama! I heard him... Every word!"
"Well, be that as it may, best we beware,
And, for the moment, spend our time in prayer."
    When comes the morrow, as you might suppose,
Still are they arguing the ayes and noes,
The thises and the thats of their adventure.
Come night, and once again our horning wencher
Pays them a visit; blares with one of those
Frighteningest of voices: "Infidel!
Thou faithless woman! Thou who wouldst defy
God, thy creator! Fly, O thou most fell!
Fly to the hermit! Hear? Else must thou die!"
"You see, mama?" cries daughter in reply.
"My God, let's go seek out the saintly man.
For so fear I your death that I would run
Headlong to find him, fast as fast I can."
Answers the mother: "Let his will be done!"
Little the belle suspects, and still less knows,
What plans the hermit has for her. However,
Quickly she goes to don her Sunday clothes—
Blouse, silvered chain, fine velvet ribbon bows:
Damsel would please; where-, when-, and whomsoever.
Off in his lair the wretch of double face
Prepares to meet his prey this night. The place?

Le pûssent voir comme un brave Soldat
Le foüet en main, toûjours en un estat
De penitence, et de tirer des flâmes
Quelque defunct puny pour ses mesfaits,
Faisant si bien en frappant tout auprés,
Qu'on crust oüir cinquante disciplines.
Il n'ouvrit pas à nos deux Pelerines
Du premier coup, et pendant un moment
Chacune peut l'entrevoir s'escrimant
Du saint outil. Enfin la porte s'ouvre,
Mais ce ne fut d'un bon Miserere.
Le Papelard conre-fait l'estonné.
Tout en tremblant la Veuve luy découvre,
Non sans rougir, le cas comme il estoit.
A six pas d'eux la fillette attendoit
Le resultat, qui fut que nostre Hermite
Les renvoya, fit le bon hipocrite.
Je crains, dit-il, les ruses du malin:
Dispensez-moy, le sexe feminin
Ne doit avoit en ma Celulle entrée.
Jamais de moy S. Pere ne naistra.
La Veuve dit toute déconfortée:
Jamais de vous? et pourquoy ne fera?
Elle ne pût en tirer autre chose.
En s'en allant la fillette disoit:
Helas! Maman, nos pechez en sont cause.
La nuit revient, et l'une et l'autre estoit
Au premier somme, alors que l'hipocrite
Et son cornet font bruire la maison.
Il leur cria toûjours du mesme ton:
Retournez voir Luce le saint Hermite.

His monkly niche, the outer wall of which
Sports now a subtle slit, so that both *mère*
And *fille*, when once they venture there,
Will spy him, gallant brave—his scourging switch
Firmly in hand—with penitential air,
Whipping himself in feverish flagellation
To save some soul from hellfire and damnation.
And when, indeed, in time, the pilgrim pair
Arrive at their ungodly destination,
Sure is Frère Luce to keep them at the door
So that they both may watch as, more and more,
He flails and fences with his holy tool.
Opening up at last, aloof and cool
Is his demeanor, as he stands dissembling.
Less than the time it takes for one Hail Mary—4
And there he is, our vile voluptuary,
Pretending great surprise. The widow—trembling,
Blushing—explains the situation, while,
Six paces back, her daughter waits as he
Gives grudging ear. Result? Our pharisee
Fends off the pair. Says he, mouth filled with guile:
"I fear the Devil's wiles. Pardon, I pray,
God's humble servant. But, sore though it vex
And disoblige you, yet the female sex
Never must foul my chaste abode. Away!
From me shall spring no pope!" "No pope?" "Nay, nay!"
And he would say no more. "Alas, alack,
Mama!" the daughter whines. "Our sins, I warrant,
Must be the cause!" Well, our abhorrent
Hypocrite, as you might have guessed, came back.
That night, with horn in hand, he loosed another

Je l'ay changé, retournez dés demain.
Les voilà donc derechef en chemin.
Pour ne tirer plus en long cette Histoire,
Il les receut. La Mere s'en alla,
Seule s'entend, la fille demeura,
Tout doucement il vous l'apprivoisa,
Luy prit d'abord son joly bras d'yvoire,
Puis s'approcha, puis en vint au baiser,
Puis aux beautez que l'on cache à la veüe,
Puis le Galant vous la mit toute nuë,
Comme s'il eust voulu la baptiser.
O Papelars! qu'on se trompe à vos mines!
Tant luy donna du retour de Matines,
Que maux de cœur vinrent premierement,
Et maux de cœur chassez, Dieu sçait comment.
En fin finalle, une certaine enflure
La contraignit d'alonger sa ceinture:
Mais en cachette, et sans en avertir
Le forge-Pape, encore moins la Mere.
Elle craignoit qu'on ne la fist partir:
Le jeu d'Amour commençoit à luy plaire.
Vous me direz: D'où luy vint tant d'esprit?
D'où? de ce jeu, c'est l'arbre de science.
Sept mois entiers la Galande attendit;
Elle allegua son peu d'experience.

    Dés que la Mere eut indice certain
De sa grossesse, elle luy fit soudain
Trousser bagage, et remercia l'Hoste.
Luy de sa part rendit grace au Seigneur
Qui soulageoit son pauvre serviteur.
Puis au départ il leur dit que sans faute,

Torrent of thunderous phrase, as both the mother
And daughter slept. "Return! Return, I bid ye,
To Luce, tomorrow!... Luce, your saintly brother.
For now repents he of the ill he did ye."
And so they go. Now, to cut short my story:
He lets them in... Receives them both... Perforce,
The widow leaves... The daughter stays, of course,
Soon to be plied and handled *con amore*.
First he approaches, gently strokes her arms—
Fair, ivory arms; then plants a gentle kiss;
Then, gentler still, fondles those secret charms
That maids demurely hide from view. With this,
Our pious fraud strips bare the widow's daughter—
Though not to christen her with holy water!
(O rakes in zealots' clothing! Fie, messieurs!)
So often sing they matins, lauds, and primes,
That morning sickness visits her betimes:
Retching and such. When it has done with her
And goes away—though God alone knows why—
Soon she begins to wear her apron high.
But secretly. For much would she prefer,
In fact, not to inform her pope-begetter;
Or, for that matter, even less mama.
For now she feared the latter would not let her
Longer remain to sing love's fa-la-la.
Clearly the sport had come to please. "But how,"
You ask, "did one so simple find such wit?"
How? It's the sport itself that teaches!... Now,
Full seven months, and yet will she avow
That still she needs more time to master it!
    The widow, when she guesses her condition,

Moyennant Dieu, l'enfant viendroit à bien.
Gardez pourtant, Dame, de faire rien
Qui puisse nuire à vostre geniture.
Ayez grand soin de cette Creature,
Car tout bon-heur vous en arrivera.
Vous regnerez, serez la Signora,
Ferez monter aux grandeurs tous les vostres,
Princes les uns, et grands Seigneurs les autres.
Vos cousins Ducs, Cardinaux vos Neveux:
Places, Chasteaux, tant pour vous que pour eux
Ne manqueront en aucune maniere,
Non plus que l'eau qui coule en la riviere.
Leur ayant fait cette prediction,
Il leur donna sa benediction.
   La Signora, de retour chez sa Mere,
S'entretenoit jour et nuit du S. Pere,
Preparoit tout, luy faisoit des beguins:
Au demeurant prenoit tous les matins
La couple d'œufs, attendoit en liesse
Ce qui viendroit d'une telle grossesse.
Mais ce qui vint destruisit les Chasteaux,
Fit avorter les Mitres, les Chapeaux,
Et les grandeurs de toute la famille.
La Signora mit au monde une fille.

Comes, thanks their host for carrying out his mission,
Packs up her things to take her home. And he,
In turn, offers the Lord his thanks most fervent
For granting solace to his humble servant.
As off they go, our hermit debauchee
Tells them that, with God's grace, most surely she
Will come to term. "But treat, I pray, with care
The fruit within your womb. For it will be
Source of great power and pelf beyond compare.
Madame—a fine *signora*—shall bestow
Titles and riches on her kith and kin—
Cardinals, dukes—with elegant châteaux
For them (and her, forsooth!) to reign therein.
In short, wealth like the waters of the rivers!"
Finishing his prediction, he delivers
His blessing on the pair, and they take leave.
  Back home the fine *signora*, morn and eve,
Talks only of His Holiness a-borning;
Knits him his bonnets; eats two eggs each morning;[5]
Awaits with joy what her *grossesse* will bring...
Alas, abortive dreams! With little warning,
Royalty, titles, riches: everything—
Miters, châteaux—all vanished in a whirl:
Our fine *signora* had a baby girl.

The Hermit

Le Bast

Un Peintre estoit, qui jaloux de sa femme,
Allant aux champs luy peignit un baudet
Sur le nombril, en guise de cachet.
Un sien confrere amoureux de la Dame,
La va trouver, et l'asne efface net;
Dieu sçait comment; puis un autre en remet
Au mesme endroit, ainsi que l'on peut croire.
A celuy-cy, par faute de memoire,
Il mit un Bast; l'autre n'en avoit point.
L'Epoux revient, veut s'éclaircir du poinct.
Voyez, mon fils, dit la bonne commere,
L'asne est témoin de ma fidelité.
—Diantre soit fait, dit l'Epoux en colere,
Et du témoin, et de qui l'a basté.

The Packsaddle

A painter, jealous of his wife, there was,
Who, off to tend his crops, thought he had cause
To paint her navel with an ass. However,
One of his friends, who loved her with a passion,
Came and rubbed off the ass in proper fashion
(God knows I needn't tell you how!); then, clever,
Painted another in the selfsame place.
But he forgets the first one had no saddle,
And paints the second one with packs a-straddle.
Husband returns, examines wife apace...
"You see," says she, "how faithful I am to you?
Witness my ass, proof of the homage due you!"
"Your ass," he cries, enraged, "can go to hell.
And he, by God, who saddled it, as well!"[1]

Le Baiser rendu

Guillot passoit avec sa mariée.
Un Gentil-homme à son gré la trouvant:
Qui t'a, dit-il, donné telle Epousée?
Que je la baise à la charge d'autant.
—Bien volontiers, dit Guillot à l'instant.
Elle est, Monsieur, fort à vostre service.
Le Monsieur donc fait alors son office;
En appuyant; Perronnelle en rougit.
Huit jours aprés ce Gentil-homme prit
Femme à son tour: à Guillot il permit
Mesme faveur. Guillot tout plein de zele:
Puisque Monsieur, dit-il, est si fidele,
J'ay grand regret et je suis bien fâché
Qu'ayant baisé seulement Perronnelle,
Il n'ait encore avec elle couché.

The Kiss Returned

A certain noble found Guillot's new bride
Much to his taste. "My man," said he, "I pray
You let me kiss your lovely wife. One day
I'll pay you back in kind!" Guillot replied:
"Monsieur may do his heart's desire with her."
Whereat the squire, with lusty buss, caresses
Poor Perronnelle, who, blushing, acquiesces.
Next week it happens that our gallant sir
Takes him a wife as well, and lets Guillot—
True to his word, indeed—come and bestow
A kiss in turn. The peasant, with much zest,
Acquits himself: many the "ah" and "oh"…
But then: "Damnation!" and he beats his breast.
"Since monsieur keeps his promise… Well, instead,
Why didn't he take my Perronnelle to bed?"

Epigramme

Alis malade, et se sentant presser,
Quelqu'un luy dit: il faut se confesser:
Voulez-vous pas mettre en repos vostre ame?
—Ouy je le veux, luy répondit la Dame:
Qu'à Pere André l'on aille de ce pas;
Car il entend d'ordinaire mon cas.
Un Messager y court en diligence;
Sonne au Convent de toute sa puissance.
Qui venez-vous demander? luy dit-on.
—C'est Pere André, celuy qui d'ordinaire
Entend Alis dans sa confession.
—Vous demandez, reprit alors un Frere,
Le Pere André le Confesseur d'Alis?
Il est bien loin: Helas le pauvre Pere
Depuis dix ans confesse en Paradis.

Epigram

Alis, as she lay ill and well-nigh dying,
Hears someone say: "Madame, I think it best
That you confess your sins and set to rest
Your soul." "I think so too," sighed she, replying.
"Go send at once for Père André. For he,
And he alone, always confesses me."
Messenger runs to monastery, flying;
Arrives; rings loud and long. At length, a brother
Opens and asks: "Whom do you wish?" "No other
Than Père André. Alis is sick, God bless her,
And prays he come, as always, to confess her."
"So? You would speak, you say, with Père André?"
Answers the monk. "The one who always hears
Madame's confession?... 'Always,' did you say?...
Where, sire? In heaven? He's dead these last ten years."

Comment l'esprit vient aux filles

Il est un jeu divertissant sur tous,
Jeu dont l'ardeur souvent se renouvelle:
Ce qui m'en plaist, c'est que tant de cervelle
N'y fait besoin, et ne sert de deux cloux.
Or devinez comment ce jeu s'appelle.

Vous y jouez; comme-aussi faisons nous:
Il divertit et la laide et la belle:
Soit jour, soit nuit, à toute heure il est doux;
Car on y voit assez clair sans chandelle.
Or devinez comment ce jeu s'appelle.

Le beau du jeu n'est connu de l'époux;
C'est chez l'Amant que ce plaisir excelle:
De regardans pour y juger des coups,
Il n'en faut point, jamais on n'y querelle.
Or devinez comment ce jeu s'appelle.

Qu'importe-t'il? sans s'arrester au nom,
Ny badiner là dessus d'avantage,
Je vais encor vous en dire un usage,
Il fait venir l'esprit et la raison.
Nous le voyons en mainte bestiole.
Avant que Lise allast en cette école,
Lise n'estoit qu'un miserable oyson.
Coudre et filer c'estoit son exercice;
Non pas le sien, mais celuy de ses doigts;
Car que l'esprit eust part à cét office,
Ne le croyez; il n'estoit nuls emplois

How Women Get Their Wit

There is a pastime—mankind's favorite—
A sport that sets the passion-fires aflame.
What I like best about it, I admit,
Is that, to play, our head counts not a whit.
Now tell me, can you guess this pastime's name?

    You play; so do we all: belle—damsel, dame—
And ugly lass alike delight in it.
By day, by night, its joys are quite the same:
However dark, our way is amply lit.
Now tell me, can you guess this pastime's name?

    Lovers—not husbands!—are by far most fit
To revel in the pleasures of this game.
Nor need we arbiters for it: to wit,
To judge good strokes from ill, and "Foul!" exclaim.[1]
Now tell me, can you guess this pastime's name?

    So much for what it's called. Let's prate no more
Thereon, nor twit and banter on that score.
Rather will I discover by the by
How women get their wit therefrom. For I
Know many a charming little female creature
Who got her reason from no other teacher!
Witness herewith the tale of one of them.
Before she learned this master's lessons, Lise
Was but a silly goose, it must be said,
With never a proper thought 'twixt ear and ear—
Nor knowing aught save needle, yarn, and thread:
Skills of the fingers, not the head, I fear—

Où Lise peust avoir l'ame occupée:
Lise songeoit autant que sa poupée.
Cent fois le jour sa Mere luy disoit:
Va-t'en chercher de l'esprit mal-heureuse.
La pauvre fille aussi-tost s'en alloit
Chez les voisins, affligée et honteuse,
Leur demandant où se vendoit l'esprit.
On en rioit; à la fin l'on luy dit:
Allez trouver Pere Bonaventure,
Car il en a bonne provision.
Incontinent la jeune creature
S'en va le voir, non sans confusion:
Elle craignoit que ce ne fust dommage
De détourner ainsi tel personnage.
Me voudroit-il faire de tels presens
A moy qui n'ay que quatorze ou quinze ans?
Vaux-je cela? disoit en soy la belle.
Son innocence augmentoit ses appas:
Amour n'avoit à son croc de pucelle
Dont il creust faire un aussi bon repas.
Mon Reverend, dit-elle au beat homme,
Je viens vous voir; des personnes m'ont dit
Qu'en ce Couvent on vendoit de l'esprit:
Vôtre plaisir seroit-il qu'à credit
J'en pusse avoir? non pas pour grosse somme;
A gros achapt mon tresor ne suffit:
Je reviendray s'il m'en faut d'avantage:
Et cependant prenez cecy pour gage.
A ce discours, je ne sçais quel anneau,
Qu'elle tiroit de son doigt avec peine,
Ne venant point, le Pere dit: tout beau;

And thinking little more than did her doll!
Her mother nagged and chafed at her withal:
"Go, ninny, get some wit!" And Lise, poor dear,
Ran straightway to the neighbors' house, distressed;
Asked where to buy some wit... "Where is it sold?"
At first they chaffed and chortled, uncontrolled;
But, finally, told her: "If you want the best,
Go see the friar. He's got enough to spare."
So off she hies her to the reverend *père*,
Though not, indeed, without misgiving lest
A personage of his imposing station
Be importuned by such a brash request.
"What?" wonders Lise with doubt and trepidation,
"Why should he waste his time on such as me,
Mere lass of fifteen years and low degree?
Ah no, alack, alas! I fear I'll not
Be worth one whit of all that wit he's got!"
Love, in his larder, keeps no fare, forsooth,
No meal more meet or tenderer to the tooth,
Than this fair virgin, fittest for the feast.
Her innocence and artlessness increased
Young Lise's charms and beauty manyfold
As she approached the priest. "*Mon père*," said she,
"They've sent me here to buy some wit. I'm told
You've some for sale. Now, if you would agree
To sell a bit, and trust me for the sum,
Then, if it please you, I should like to buy it.
Mind you, I can't but much... Enough to try it.
If I want more, then I can always come
And get me some. As for the price... Well, here,
Take this for now..." So saying, she vainly tries
To pull a ring from off her hand. "Ah!" sighs

Nous pourvoirons à ce qui vous ameine
Sans exiger nul salaire de vous:
Il est marchande et marchande, entre nous;
A l'une on vend ce qu'à l'autre l'on donne.
Entrez icy; suivez moy hardiment;
Nul ne nous voit, aucun ne nous entend,
Tous sont au chœur; le portier est personne
Entierement à ma devotion;
Et ces murs ont de la discretion.
Elle le suit; ils vont à sa Cellule.
Mon Reverend la jette sur un lit,
Veut la baiser; la pauvrette recule
Un peu la teste; et l'innocente dit:
Quoy c'est ainsi qu'on donne de l'esprit?
—Et vrayment oüy, repart sa Reverence;
Puis il luy met la main sur le teton:
Encore ainsi?—vrayment oüy; comment donc?
La belle prend le tout en patience:
Il suit sa pointe; et d'encor en encor
Tousjours l'esprit s'insinuë et s'avance,
Tant et si bien qu'il arrive à bon port.
Lise rioit du succés de la chose.
Bonaventure à six moments de là
Donne d'esprit une seconde dose.
Ce ne fut tout, une autre succeda;
La charité du beau Pere estoit grande.
Et bien, dit-il, que vous semble du jeu?
—A nous venir l'esprit tarde bien peu,
Reprit la belle; et puis elle demande:
Mais s'il s'en va?—s'il s'en va? nous verrons;
D'autres secrets se mettent en usage.

Our pious sire. "Tut tut! No need, my dear...
No need... Here shall you have your fill of wit.
Nor shall you spend one blessèd sou for it.
For, though some ladies of our clientele
Must pay in full for what we have to sell,
Some—*entre nous*, like you—may have it free.[2]
Now then, I pray you follow me, *ma belle*.
Off to my cell, where we, in privacy,
May tend to our affair. Nor need you fear,
Ma chère, the spying eye or prying ear:
The porter, faithfulest of sycophants,
Hears nought, I warrant, that he ought not hear.
As for the rest, they're off chanting their chants.
So come." She follows, and the pair repair
To where the monkly troupe reside. Once there,
Lo! Suddenly he throws her to his bed
And goes to kiss her lips. She turns her head
Innocently aside, draws back a bit,
And asks: "Ah so, *mon père?* Is this the way
To give me wit?" To which he answers: "Yea,
Verily!" as he lays upon her tit
(Or teat, if you insist) a lustful hand.
"And this?" "Yes, that as well. And this, and..." "And?"
"And... And..." And on he goes, dispensing wit
With no resistance from our *demoiselle*,
Who takes much pleasure. And he does so well
That he dispenses all he has of it.
All? Well, not quite. Not really all, that is...
For, with that saintly charity of his,
Soon he metes out a second dose, still greater;
Then yet a third, firmly to inculcate her.[3]
"How fancy you our sport?" he says. Says she

—N'en cherchez point, dit Lise, davantage;
De celuy-cy nous nous contenterons.
—Soit fait, dit-il, nous recommencerons
Au pis aller, tant et tant qu'il suffise.
Le pis aller sembla le mieux à Lise.
Le secret mesme encor se repeta
Par le Pater; il aimoit cette dance.
Lise luy fait une humble reverence;
Et s'en retourne en songeant à cela.
Lise songer! quoy dé-ja Lise songe!
Elle fait plus, elle cherche un mensonge,
Se doutant bien qu'on luy demanderoit,
Sans y manquer, d'où ce retard venoit.
Deux jours aprés sa compagne Nanette
S'en vient la voir: pendant leur entretien
Lise révoit: Nanette comprit bien,
Comme elle estoit clair-voyante et finette,
Que Lise alors ne révoit pas pour rien.
Elle fait tant, tourne tant son amie,
Que celle-cy luy declare le tout.
L'autre n'estoit à l'oüir endormie.
Sans rien cacher, Lise de bout en bout
De point en point luy conte le mystere,
Dimensions de l'esprit du beau Pere,
Et les encor, enfin tout le Phœbé.
Mais vous, dit-elle, apprenez-nous de grace
Quand et par qui l'esprit vous fut donné.
Anne reprit: puis qu'il faut que je fasse
Un libre aveu, c'est vostre frere Alain
Qui m'a donné de l'esprit un matin.
—Mon frere Alain! Alain! s'ecria Lise,

In turn: "Wit seems to come quite easily.
To me, at least. But I'm afraid lest, later,
It leave me just as fast!" "Fear not," says he.
"For we have other ways to remedy
Such a misfortune." "Other ways?" she cries.
"Let's keep to this one! Why do otherwise?"
"Well, if we must..." "We must," insists fair Lise,
Who wants no part of other remedies.
"So be it!" says the friar, who, yet again,
Ekes out a jot more wit... And then, amen,
A humble curtsy, and she's out the door,
Thinking, reflecting on his little dance...
What? Lise was thinking? Thinking? Lise?... What's more,
She even thought that, given the circumstance,
She ought invent some tale, some fabrication,
The better to explain her long delay
If one should ask. And, sure enough, next day,
She found herself, in fact, in conversation
With friend Nanette. The latter was surprised
To see her much absorbed in contemplation;
And, well endowed of wit herself, surmised
That witless Lise, to be so deep in thought,
Would not, indeed, be musing thus for nought.
Whereat she prods, until the newly witted
Reveals the deed, without one stroke omitted;
Everything, start to finish, bit by bit,
Unto the measure of the *bon père*'s wit.[4]
"But," counters Lise, "please, pray you, tell me, too,
Who first bestowed his load of wit on you?"
"The first?" replies Nanette. "Well, I admit...
Alain it was, one morning, who—" "Come now!"
Cries Lise. "My brother? Wit? But how?

Alain mon frere! ah je suis bien surprise;
Il n'en a point; comme en donneroit-il?
—Sotte, dit l'autre, helas tu n'en sçais guere:
Apprens de moy que pour pareille affaire
Il n'est besoin que l'on soit si subtil.
Ne me crois-tu? sçache le de ta mere;
Elle est experte au fait dont il s'agit;
Si tu ne veux, demande au voisinage;
Sur ce point là l'on t'aura bien-tost dit:
Vivent les sots pour donner de l'esprit.
Lise s'en tint à ce seul témoignage,
Et ne crût pas devoir parler de rien.
Vous voyez donc que je disois fort bien
Quand je disois que ce jeu là rend sage.

Alain? Impossible! That nit? That clot?
How could he give you what he hasn't got?"
"Poor sot!" Nanette is quick to chide, retorting.
"Be it your friar, be it Alain your brother,
Man needs no subtle art for such disporting.
So? Do you doubt my word? Go ask your mother.
She knows whereof I speak, believe you me.
Or ask the neighbors round. I guarantee
That one and all are of a single mind:
Long live our louts, who, witless though they be,
Deal us a dole of wit, unwittingly!"
But Lise demurs, grown wisely disinclined
To bruit her secret now to whomsoever.
See? As I said: that sport turns women clever.

How Women Get Their Wit

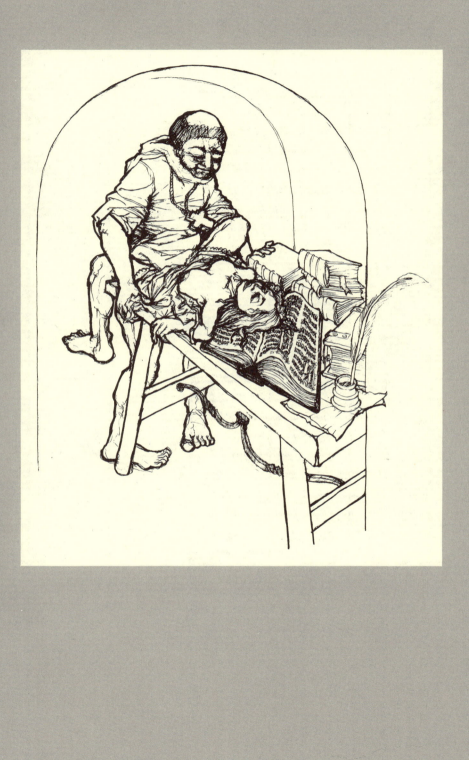

L'Abbesse

L'exemple sert, l'exemple nuit aussi:
Lequel des deux doit l'emporter icy,
Ce n'est mon fait; l'un dira que l'Abbesse
En usa bien, l'autre au contraire mal,
Selon les gens: bien ou mal je ne laisse
D'avoir mon compte, et montre en general,
Par ce que fit tout un troupeau de Nones,
Qu'oüailles sont la pluspart des personnes;
Qu'il en passe une, il en passera cent;
Tant sur les gens est l'exemple puissant.
Je le repete, et dis, vaille que vaille,
Le monde n'est que franche moutonnaille.
Du premier coup ne croyez que l'on aille
A ses perils le passage sonder;
On est long-temps à s'entreregarder;
Les plus hardis ont ils tenté l'affaire,
Le reste suit, et fait ce qu'il void faire.
Qu'un seul mouton se jette en la riviere,
Vous ne verrez nulle ame moutonniere
Rester au bord, tous se noyront à tas.
Maître François en conte un plaisant cas.
Amy Lecteur, ne te déplaira pas,
Si sursoyant ma principale histoire
Je te remets cette chose en memoire.
Panurge alloit l'oracle consulter.
Il navigeoit, ayant dans la cervelle
Je ne sçais quoy qui vint l'inquieter.
Dindenaut passe; et medaille l'appelle
De vray cocu. Dindenaut dans sa nef

The Abbess

Example helps; example harms as well.
My purpose, with this tale, is not to tell
If harm or help was wrought thereby. For, some
Will think our abbess profited therefrom;
Others would sooner say a fate most fell
Befell this mother of her flock. For me,
"Helpful or harmful" really matters not.
Rather I merely wish to show, by what
Occurred amongst a certain company
Of good and holy sisters—that is, nuns—
That convent-folk are human. What the ones
Will do, so will the others imitate.
People are sheep, I think it fair to state.
Often, if I dare make comparisons,
The first ones test the water, whilst the pack,
In fear and doubt, glancing about, hang back
Until the leaders take the leap. Then will
The others follow, one and all; until
Each sheep, quitting the shore—alas, alack!—
Sinks to the bottom, drowned, to leap no more.
Maître François (you know that sobriquet
Of our renowned tale-teller Rabelais)
Tells us a tale that proves my point. Before
I carry on with mine, dear reader, let
Me tell his yet again, lest you forget.
Panurge was on a voyage to consult
The oracle—distraught, I know not why—
When Dindenaut the merchant cried: "My, my!
Look at the proper cuckold!" The result?

Menoit moutons. Vendez m'en un, dit l'autre.
—Voire, reprit Dindenaut, l'amy nostre,
Penseriez-vous qu'on pust venir à chef
D'assez priser ny vendre telle aumaille?
Panurge dit: nôtre ami, coûte et vaille,
Vendez m'en un pour or ou pour argent.
Un fut vendu. Panurge incontinant
Le jette en mer; et les autres de suivre.
Au diable l'un, à ce que dit le livre,
Qui demeura. Dindenaut au collet
Prend un belier, et le bellier l'entraisne.
Adieu mon homme: il va boire au godet.
Or revenons: ce prologue me meine
Un peu bien loin. J'ay posé des l'abord
Que tout exemple est de force tres-grande:
Et ne me suis écarté par trop fort
En rapportant la Moutonniere bande:
Car nôtre histoire est d'oüailles encor.
Une passa, puis une autre, et puis une:
Tant qu'à passer s'entre-pressant chacune
On vid enfin celle qui les gardoit
Passer aussi: c'est en gros tout le conte:
Voicy comment en détail on le conte.

    Certaine Abbesse un certain mal avoit,
Pasles couleurs nommé parmy les filles:
Mal dangereux, et qui des plus gentilles
Détruit l'éclat, fait languir les attraits.
Nôtre malade avoit la face blesme
Tout justement comme un Saint de Caresme,
Bonne d'ailleurs, et gente à cela prés.

Panurge, insulted, says he wants to buy
One of the sheep the former is transporting.
"One of my sheep?" jeers Dindenaut, retorting.
"The likes of you could never pay its value!"
"Pish tush," replies Panurge. "I'll give you gold.
Or silver if you wish. What say you? Shall you
Sell me but one?" " 'Tis done!" And one was sold.
Wherewith Panurge proceeds to seize it, heave it
Into the sea. The rest—would you believe it?—
Leaping behind, each one, follow the leader;
Until, as Rabelais informs the reader,
But one remains. That lusty ram, the last,
Drags Dindenaut himself—clutching him fast,
To hold him back—into the drink. Adieu...
Now, with no further (as one says) ado,
Let me resume my tale, too long deferred.
Yet is my lengthy prologue, in a word
(Or two, or three) most *à propos*: I too
Will talk about a flock as well; although
Human, my sheep. Still, followers, just so,
Chasing the first, until, little by little,
All finally take the plunge; and even, lo!
Their shepherdess. Such is my tale *en gros*.
Now let me tell it with each jot and tittle.

A certain abbess, gaunter by the day,
Was ailing with "the pallor," as they say—
Dangerous ill, and one that soon erases
The bloom of beauty from the fairest faces.
Pallid and wan, but comely save for same,
Good sister languished until she became
The very picture of a saint ascetic.

La faculté sur ce point consultée,
Aprés avoir la chose examinée,
Dit que bien-tost Madame tomberoit
En fievre lente, et puis qu'elle mourroit.
Force sera que cette humeur la mange;
A moins que de... l'amoins est bien étrange;
A moins enfin qu'elle n'ayt à souhait
Compagnie d'homme. Hipocrate ne fait
Choix de ses mots, et tant tourner ne sçait.
Jesus, reprit toute scandalisée
Madame Abbesse: hé que dites-vous là?
Fi.—Nous disons, repartit à cela
La faculté, que pour chose assurée
Vous en mourrez, à moins d'un bon galant:
Bon le faut-il, c'est un poinct important:
Autre que bon n'est icy suffisant:
Et si bon n'est deux en prendrez Madame.
Ce fut bien pis; non pas que dans son Ame
Ce bon ne fust par elle souhaité:
Mais le moyen que sa Communauté
Luy vist sans peine approuver telle chose?
Honte souvent est de dommage cause.
Sœur Agnés dit: Madame croyez les.
Un tel remede est chose bien mauvaise;
S'il a le goust meschant à beaucoup prés
Comme la mort. Vous faites cent secrets,
Faut-il qu'un seul vous choque et vous déplaise?
—Vous en parlez, Agnés, bien à vostre aise,
Reprit l'Abesse: or ça, par vostre Dieu,
Le feriez-vous? mettez-vous en mon lieu.
—Oüy-dea Madame; et dis bien davantage:

Convoked therefor, Doctores Medicinae—
Studying her condition with their keen eye—
Decreed that no balm, physic, or emetic
Would bring her back to health; in tone prophetic
Stating that, by the ague thus consumed,
Most surely must she die. And thus they doomed—
Ordained—her to expire. That is, unless...
Unusual their "unless," I must confess:
Unless, in fact, she dally at her leisure
And heart's content with man, and do his pleasure.
(The cure, as posed in language Hippocratic,
Is, I assure you, rather more emphatic.)
"Sweet Jesus!" cries the nun. "Misery me!
What remedy is this?" "Fie, fie, *ma sœur*,"
Reply the Magi of the Faculty,
In no uncertain terms condemning her:
"A man, or die! And not some lowly cur!
A good one, sister, must your gallant be,
Well versed in matters such. If not, we fear
You needs must, for as much, take two. You hear?"
Now, let it not be thought that she, forsooth,
Foreswore said good and gallant cavalier
Deep in her heart of hearts. But how, in truth,
Could she allow the nuns, amazed thereat,
To think that she approved a thing like that?
Often is shame the source of wretchedness.
"*Ma mère*," observed one sister, Sœur Agnès,
"Though foul the cure, far worse, no doubt, is dying.
Full fivescore secrets must you have, no less:
Will one more really be so horrifying?
Best you do what they tell you to." Replying,

Vostre santé m'est chere jusque là
Que s'il faloit pour vous souffrir cela,
Je ne voudrois que dans ce témoignage
D'affection pas une de çeans
Me devançast. Mille remerciemens
A sœur Agnes donnés par son Abbesse,
La faculté dit àdieu la dessus;
Et protesta de ne revenir plus.
Tout le Couvent se trouvoit en tristesse,
Quand sœur Agnes qui n'estoit de ce lieu
La moins sensée, au reste bonne lame,
Dit à ses sœurs: tout ce qui tient Madame
Est seulement belle honte de Dieu.
Par charité n'en est-il point quelqu'une
Pour luy monstrer l'exemple et le chemin?
Cét avis fût approuvé de chacune:
On l'applaudit, il court de main en main.
Pas une n'est qui monstre en ce dessein
De la froideur, soit None, soit Nonette,
Mere Prieure, ancienne, ou discrete.
Le billet trotte: on fait venir des gens
De tout guise, et des noirs, et des blancs,
Et des tannez. L'escadron, dit l'histoire,
Ne fut petit, ny comme l'on peut croire
Lent à monstrer de sa part le chemin.
Ils ne cedoient à pas une Nonain
Dans le desir de faire que Madame
Ne fust honteuse, ou bien n'eust dans son ame
Tel recipé possible à contre-cœur.
De ses brebis à peine la premiere
A fait le saut, qu'il suit une autre sœur.

The abbess sighed. "Ah, yes. It's well and good
To make so free, Agnès, with your advice.
But let me ask you, sister, if you would,
Yourself, by God, make such a sacrifice!"
"Indeed, *ma mère*! And more! So dear to me
Is my abbess's health that, in a trice,
Gladly would I endure such remedy.
Nor—and of this you may be sure—would I
Let any nun herein forestall thereby
My zeal in doing so." Profuse, sincere
The thanks the abbess proffers her; whereon,
Bidding adieu, the Magi disappear,
Professing never to return anon.
Chagrined were all the sisters, sore distressed;
Whilst Sœur Agnès, nowise the foolishest
Amongst them—nay, a canny nun—deplored
Her scruples: "Fearful is our abbess lest
The curious cure proposed offend the Lord.
But, if one nun would show the way... One nun,
By pity moved, and willing to afford
The solace of example... Surely, one...?"
With that, first one... then two... then three and four
Offer their services. Then more and more...
A score... The blessèd lot! And when the word
Goes out, how many a monkish soul is stirred
To come and help: brothers of every order—
A horde, in fact—all eager to accord her
That "solace of example" that Agnès
Had urged her saintly sisters to afford her.
And, selfless, so they do, with much largesse,
All bent on proving that the doctors' cure

Une troisiesme entre dans la carriere.
Nulle ne veut demeurer en arriere.
Presse se met pour n'estre la derniere
Qui feroit voir son zele et sa ferveur
A mere Abbesse. Il n'est aucune oüaille
Qui ne s'y jette; ainsi que les moutons
De Dindenaut dont tantost nous parlions
S'alloient jetter chez la gent portécaille.
Que diray plus? enfin l'impression
Qu'avoit l'Abbesse encontre ce remede,
Sage renduë à tant d'exemples cede.
Un jouvenceau fait l'operation
Sur la malade. Elle redevient rose,
Œillet, aurore, et si quelque autre chose
De plus riant se peut imaginer.
O doux remede, ô remede à donner,
Remede ami de mainte Creature,
Ami des gens, ami de la nature,
Ami de tout, poinct d'honneur excepté.
Poinct d'honneur est une autre maladie:
Dans ses écrits Madame faculté
N'en parle point. Que de maux en la vie!

Need cause no shame and no discomfiture;
Each spotless lamb, intent upon her mission
To put to rights the abbess's condition,
Bounding into the fray, with single mind,
Lest any—heaven forbid!—be left behind
To let her conscience languish in contrition.
As when those sheep of Dindenaut's, inclined—
One-minded flock—by water's edge converging,
To leap, each one in turn, with no "Panurge-ing,"
Into the brine. What more need I relate?
Convinced by such a widely held idea,
Our abbess yields: she'll try the panacea.
A youth was chosen, thus, to operate
Upon her; and, so fine his operation,
That soon, again, the bloom of rose, carnation—
Indeed, of dawn itself—enrobed, enwrapped her.
(Or may you find, mayhap, an image apter.)
O cure of universal application!
Sweet cure, for all the ills that may betide
Our kind; save one: our overweening pride.
Ah, pride! that illness that, uncured by love,
Our Medicasters make no mention of!

The Abbess

Le Psautier

Nones souffrez pour la derniere fois
Qu'en ce recueuil malgré moy je vous place.
De vos bons tours les contes ne sont froids.
Leur avanture a ne sçais quelle grace
Qui n'est ailleurs: ils emportent les voix.
Encore un donc, et puis c'en seront trois.
Trois? je faux d'un; c'en seront au moins quatre.
Contons-les bien. Mazet le compagnon;
L'Abbesse ayant besoin d'un bon garçon
Pour la guerir d'un mal opiniâtre;
Ce conte-cy qui n'est le moins fripon;
Quant à sœur Jeanne ayant fait un poupon,
Je ne tiens pas qu'il la faille rabatre.
Les voilà tous: quatre c'est conte rond.
Vous me direz: c'est une étrange affaire,
Que nous ayons tant de part en ceci.
Que voulez-vous? je n'y sçaurois que faire;
Ce n'est pas moy qui le souhaite ainsi.
Si vous teniez toûjours vostre breviaire,
Vous n'auriez rien à demesler icy.
Mais ce n'est pas vostre plus grand souci.
Passons donc viste à la presente histoire.
Dans un couvent de Nones frequentoit
Un jouvençeau friand comme on peut croire
De ces oiseaux. Telle pourtant prenoit
Goust à le voir, et des yeux le couvoit,
Luy sourioit, faisoit la complaisante,
Et se disoit sa tres-humble servante,

The Psalter

Good sisters, though against my will, I pray
You let me make you—for this one last time,
Herein again—the subject of my rhyme.
Your canny wit and wile give pleasure—nay,
Utterly charm my readers, who prefer
A lusty tale about a crafty *sœur*.
So, this one now makes three... "Three," did I say?
No, wait... I err by one. I should say "four."
Let's see... The tale about our friend Mazet
Came first of all; our abbess was one more—
That nun, you may recall, who, at death's door,
Was cured by gallant's tender ministration;
Now this one, no less bawdy than the lot.
As for Sœur Jeanne, who bore that chubby tot,
Surely she too deserves consideration.[1]
And so full four in all. You say: "Blame not
Us readers for your inspiration; we
Are not at fault." But I reply: "And me?
Am I? I have no choice. I write not what
I wish, but what I know you wish to read.
If you kept to your prayer books, then, indeed,
You would have little need to read—nor I,
To write, good gentle reader, by the by—
Such tales as these. Well then, so much
For this, my peroration prefatory:
Best I get on with it and tell the story.
A youth there was of great good fortune, such
That he frequented, quite ad libitum,
A nunnery, where he would go and come

Qui pour cela d'un seul poinct n'avançoit.

Le conte dit que leans il n'estoit
Vieille ny jeune, à qui le personnage
Ne fist songer quelque chose à part soy.
Soupirs trotoient, bien voyoit le pourquoy,
Sans qu'il s'en mist en peine davantage.
Sœur Isabeau seule pour son usage
Eut le galand: elle le meritoit
Douce d'humeur, gentille de corsage,
Et n'en estant qu'à son apprentissage,
Belle de plus. Ainsi l'on l'envioit
Pour deux raisons; son amant, et ses charmes.
Dans ses amours chacune l'épioit:
Nul bien sans mal, nul plaisir sans alarmes.
Tant et si bien l'épierent les sœurs,
Qu'une nuit sombre, et propre à ces douceurs
Dont on confie aux ombres le mystere,
En sa cellule on oüit certains mots,
Certaine voix, enfin certains propos
Qui n'estoient pas sans doute en son bréviaire.
C'est le galand, ce dit-on, il est pris.
Et de courir; l'alarme est aux esprits;
L'éxaim fremit, sentinelle se pose.
On va conter en triomphe la chose
A mere Abbesse; et heurtant à grand coups
On luy cria: Madame levez-vous;
Sœur Isabelle a dans sa chambre un homme.
Vous noterez que Madame n'estoit
En oraison, ny ne prenoit son somme:
Trop bien alors dans son lit elle avoit
Messire Jean curé du voisinage.

Day in day out.[2] Now, in this aviary
Of chirping belles, the said voluptuary
Lusted to pluck some plumes. And all, in turn—
Old, young (so goes the tale)—would fairly burn
With wistful passion to be plucked. And yet,
Much though the nuns would yearn, each to be his,
For all their sighs and smiles, to their regret,
None got what all, so long, had longed to get.
Except for one, Sœur Isabelle, that is.
Of all the gaggle, far the worthiest:
A novice still; sweet-tempered, firm of breast,
Most passing fair of face. And so was she
The object of their twofold jealousy:
First, for her charms, envy of all the rest;
Second, because the beau chose her, not them.
Thus do they try, by every stratagem
At their command, to spy upon the pair
(No joy unmarred, no pleasure free from care!),
And pry so well, one night—one of those nights
Made, so it seems, to hide love's dark delights
In shadow—that the sisters, ear to door,
Hear, in her cell, not sounds of sacred rites,
But certain words, a certain voice; and more
Than their chaste ears have ever heard before.
"Him! Him!" they cackle. "Now we've caught him with her!"
And off they fly, all in a holy dither—
Leaving one sister as a sentinel—
A-flutter and a-twitter, off to tell
The holy mother: "Come, *ma mère!* Come hither!..."
And, pounding on her door: "Sœur Isabelle
Is with a man!" The abbess, I must say—

Pour ne donner aux sœurs aucun ombrage,
Elle se leve, en haste, étourdiment,
Cherche son voile, et malheureusement
Dessous sa main tombe du personnage
Le haut de chausse assez bien ressemblant
Pendant la nuit quand on n'est éclairée
A certain voile aux Nones familier,
Nommé pour lors entre-elles leur Psautier.
La voila donc de gregues affublée.
Ayant sur soy ce nouveau couvrechef,
Et s'estant fait raconter derechef
Tout le catus, elle dit irritée:
Voyez un peu la petite effrontée,
Fille du diable, et qui nous gastera
Nostre couvent; si Dieu plaist ne fera:
S'il plaist à Dieu bon ordre s'y mettra:
Vous la verrez tantost bien chapitrée.
Chapitre donc, puisque chapitre y a,
Fut assemblé. Mere Abbesse entourée
De son Senat fit venir Isabeau,
Qui s'arrosoit de pleurs tout le visage,
Se souvenant qu'un maudit jouvenceau
Venoit d'en faire un different usage.
Quoy, dit l'Abbesse, un homme dans ce lieu!
Un tel scandale en la maison de Dieu!
N'estes vous point morte de honte encore?
Qui nous a fait reçevoir parmi nous
Cette voirie? Isabeau, sçavez-vous
(Car desormais qu'icy l'on vous honore
Du nom de sœur, ne le pretendez pas)
Sçavez-vous dis-je à quoy dans un tel cas

Not sleeping, should you get the wrong idea—
Was not reciting her Ave Maria,
But was, indeed, in bed with the *curé*,
One Messire Jean; and, in a twinkling, lest
She do her flock offense, forthwith gets dressed.
But when, alas, in clumsy haste she goes
To lay her veil upon her head, she lays
Her hand instead upon the prelate's hose.
(For in the dark those breeches—her *curé's*—
Look like the veil the sisters, joking, call
Their "psalter.") Now the door swings wide, and, lo!
There stands the abbess in her odd *chapeau*,
Bidding the clucking nuns to tell her all.
"O brazen wench! The Devil's daughter, she!
To bring such shame upon our nunnery!
But things, God grant! shall be set right withal.
The chapter must be called!... Yes, I shall call
The chapter!..." And the chapter—one, two, three—
Indeed, thereon, was called summarily
To judge Sœur Isabelle, standing accused
By council and by *mère*-inquisitor;
Cheeks moist with tears; those cheeks that, just before,
Were in such different manner used—abused—
By that confounded swain. "Shame!" caterwauled
Her Holy Mothership, duly appalled:
"A man! A man, here, in this blessèd place!
This house of God! O scandal! O disgrace!
Who...? Who...?" she bawled, "Who let this strumpet in
Amongst us, here, to live in mortal sin?
You! Isabelle!... (For I no longer would
Admit you to our virtuous ranks herein—

Nostre institut condamne une meschante?
Vous l'apprendrez devant qu'il soit demain.
Parlez parlez. Lors la pauvre Nonain,
Qui jusque-là confuse et repentante
N'osoit bransler, et la veüe abbaissoit,
Leve les yeux, par bon-heur apperçoit
Le haut de chausse, à quoy toute la bande,
Par un effet d'émotion trop grande,
N'avoit pris garde, ainsi qu'on void souvent.
Ce fut hazard qu'Isabelle à l'instant
S'en apperceut. Aussi-tost la pauvrette
Reprend courage, et dit tout doucement:
Vostre Psautier a ne sçais quoy qui pend;
Raccommodez-le. Or c'estoit l'éguillette.
Assez souvent pour bouton l'on s'en sert.
D'ailleurs ce voile avoit beaucoup de l'air
D'un haut de chausse: et la jeune Nonette,
Ayant l'idée encor fraische des deux
Ne s'y méprit: Non pas que le Messire
Eust chausse faite ainsi qu'un amoureux:
Mais à peu pres; cela devoit suffire.
L'Abbesse dit: elle ose encore rire!
Quelle insolence! un peché si honteux
Ne la rend pas plus humble et plus soumise!
Veut elle point que l'on la Canonise?
Laissez mon voile esprit de Lucifer.
Songez songez, petit tison d'enfer,
Comme on pourra raccommoder vostre ame.
Pas ne finit mere Abbesse sa game
Sans sermonner et tempester beaucoup.
Sœur Isabeau luy dit encore un coup:

The saintly ranks of our good sisterhood—
By calling you *ma sœur*!) You! Do you know
To what our holy order's rules condemn
Such jades as you, and how we deal with them?
Well, trollop, you shall learn, prestissimo!
So, what have you to say?" Wherewith she fell
Finally silent, as poor Isabelle,
Raising her head at last—till then hung low—
Still as a statue, tongue-tied, sore chagrined
And much repenting that she had so sinned—
Looked up and eyed the mother's headdress (which is
That "pseudo-psalter," you recall: those breeches,
Messire *curé*'s!), which none—so terrified
And cowed were one and all—had yet espied.
She saw it quite by luck and much by chance;
But, nonetheless, under the circumstance
Her pluck returned and, softly, she replied:
"Something is hanging from your psalter." (Those
Laces that close the codpiece, I suppose.)[3]
"Alack, look to your veil, madame," she sighed.
(Psalter or breeches: she was far too clever
Not to be certain which was which, however.
For both she knows! Not that the priest has hose
Like lovers', but they'll do.) Shrieks abbess: "See?
The sinner even dares make fun of me!
Instead of humbling her into submission,
I vow she thinks transgression glorifies her,
And that, no doubt, one ought to canonize her!
Insolent harlot! Best show some contrition!
Look to your soul and let my psalter be!
Firebrand of Satan!" Thus the sermonizer,

Raccommodez vostre Psautier, Madame.
Tout le troupeau se met à regarder.
Jeunes de rire, et vieilles de gronder.
La voix manquant à nostre sermonneuse,
Qui de son troc bien faschée et honteuse,
N'eut pas le mot à dire en ce moment,
L'exaim fit voir par son bourdonnement,
Combien rouloient de diverses pensées
Dans les esprits. Enfin l'Abbesse dit:
Devant qu'on eust tant de voix ramassées,
Il seroit tard. Que chacune en son lit
S'aille remettre. A demain toute chose.
Le lendemain ne fut tenu, pour cause,
Aucun chapitre; et le jour en suivant
Tout aussi peu. Les sages du Couvent
Furent d'avis que l'on se devoit taire;
Car trop d'éclat eust pu nuire au troupeau.
On n'en vouloit à la pauvre Isabeau
Que par envie. Ainsi n'ayans pu faire
Qu'elle laschast aux autres le morceau,
Chaque Nonain, faute de jouvenceau,
Songe à pourvoir d'ailleurs à son affaire.
Les vieux amis reviennent de plus beau.
Par préciput à nostre belle on laisse
Le jeune fils; le Pasteur à l'Abbesse;
Et l'union alla jusques au poinct
Qu'on en prestoit à qui n'en avoit point.

Bellowing forth her endless litany,
Consigns her sinner to the fires of hell;
Until, at length, once more, Sœur Isabelle
Observes: "Madame, look to your veil, pray do!"
Whereat the sisters all—young, old—look too:
The former, laughing, giggling; and the latter,
Shocked at the Reverend Mother's curious dress,
Muttering with a scoff and staring at her.
Suddenly speechless now, our votaress,
Mortified and abashed at her faux pas,
Cuts short the council, as with "Hmm!" and "Ha!"
The sisters buzz their divers speculation.
Says she: "The hour grows late. As I think on it,
Best we suspend tonight's deliberation.
Tomorrow will be time. Go, sleep upon it…"
And she dismisses thus the congregation.
Tomorrow comes: no council. Next day: none.
Nor next… Nor next… When all was said and done,
To spare the order's virtuous reputation,
Nothing was done, and still less said. As for
Our Isabelle, she was but envied more.
She keeps her youth; the abbess, her *messire*.
Failing the lad, each sister soon discovers
A present beau amongst her former lovers.
So conjugal the convent atmosphere,
So loving their communion now, that many
Even lend theirs to those who haven't any.

The Psalter

La Jument du compère Pierre

Messire Jean, (c'estoit certain Curé
Qui preschoit peu sinon sur la Vendange)
Sur ce sujet, sans estre préparé,
Il triomphoit; vous eussiez dit un Ange.
Encore un poinct estoit touché de luy;
Non si souvent qu'eust voulu le Messire:
Et ce poinct là les enfans d'aujourd'huy
Sçavent que c'est, besoin n'ay de le dire.
Messire Jean tel que je le descris
Faisoit si bien que femmes et maris
Le recherchoient, estimoient sa science;
Au demeurant il n'estoit conscience
Un peu jolie, et bonne à diriger,
Qu'il ne voulust luy mesme interroger,
Ne s'en fiant aux soins de son Vicaire.
Messire Jean auroit voulu tout faire;
S'entremettoit en zelé directeur;
Alloit par tout; disant qu'un bon Pasteur
Ne peut trop bien ses oüailles connoistre,
Dont par luy mesme instruit en vouloit estre.
Parmi les gens de luy les mieux venus,
Il frequentoit chez le compere Pierre,
Bon villageois à qui pour toute terre,
Pour tout domaine, et pour tous revenus
Dieu ne donna que ses deux bras tous nus,
Et son louchet, dont pour toute ustensille
Pierre faisoit subsister sa famille.
Il avoit femme et belle et jeune encor,
Ferme sur tout; le hasle avoit fait tort

Pierre the Peasant and His Mare

A certain Messire Jean, esteemed *curé*,
Preached little save on virtues of the vine;
And that he did right well, extempore,
Goblet in hand, held high, in accents fine—
Divine, in fact.[1] He preached as well, forsooth—
Though less, alack, than he would like to do—
On subject of concern to tender youth.
(My meaning should, I think, be clear to you.)
Many a wife and husband sought him out
As their confessor, eager to confess
To one endowed with knowledge and finesse
The likes of him. And so round and about
His talents confessorial were spread;
Though more among the wives, it must be said:
For every comely-bodied soul would spur
His priestly zeal, amply conferred on her.
To each he gave his personal attention,
Eschewing his superior's intervention,
Vowing that any shepherd—and *pasteur*—
Ought know the members of his flock: each one
In intimate detail. Now, such was he
That, of his pious faithful, there was none
To whom he ministered more willingly
Than to a certain peasant, one Pierre
By name: good soul but poor beyond compare,
Whom God above had given here below
Nought but his two bare arms. His wealth? A hoe
Wherewith to eke the meagerest nourishment
For him and his. *Compère* Pierre was wed
To wife still young and pleasing; succulent

A son visage, et non à sa personne.
Nous autres gens peut-estre aurions voulu
Du délicat, ce rustiq ne m'eust plu;
Pour des Curez la paste en estoit bonne;
Et convenoit à semblables amours.
Messire Jean la regardoit toûjours
Du coin de l'œil, toûjours tournoit la teste
De son costé; comme un chien qui fait feste
Aux os qu'il void n'estre par trop chétifs;
Que s'il en void un de belle apparence,
Non dêcharné, plein encor de substance,
Il tient dessus ses regards attentifs:
Il s'inquiete, il trepigne, il remüe
Oreille et queüe; il a toûjours la veuë
Dessus cet os, et le ronge des yeux
Vingt fois devant que son palais s'en sente.
Messire Jean tout ainsi se tourmente
A cet objet pour luy delicieux.
La Villageoise estoit fort innocente,
Et n'entendoit aux façons du Pasteur
Mystere aucun; ny son regard flateur,
Ny ses presens ne touchoient Magdeleine:
Bouquets de thin, et pots de Marjolaine
Tomboient à terre: avoir cent menus soins
C'estoit parler bas-breton tout au moins.
Il s'avisa d'un plaisant stratagème.
Pierre estoit lourd, sans esprit: je crois bien
Qu'il ne se fust précipité luy mesme,
Mais par delà de luy demander rien,
C'estoit abus et tres grande sottise.

Of flesh, though tanned of skin. (Those of us bred
Today on other tastes might wish, instead—
Like me—for something somewhat daintier;
Rather less rustic, in a word, than her.
But, musing on the matters of the bed,
The cloth will find her of more apt confection!)
Subjecting her to his oblique inspection,
Our priest casts many a sidelong glance—left, right—
Like hungry hound, eyeing with much delight
A pile of bones of suitable complexion;
And, spying one, especially, that might
Be meatier than the rest, gnaws with his eyes,
Paws at the ground, with ears and tail a-twitch,
Savoring, in his mind, that morsel which
He lusts, in time, to take and make his prize.
In such wise does the eminent *curé*
Covet—nay, rather, fairly gourmandize—
The peasant's wife; who, in her naïveté,
Makes little sense of his attentivenesses,
His wheedling looks, his presents... Nought impresses
Our Magdeleine: his many a thyme bouquet,
Pots of marjoram—spurned and thrown away.
Tidbits of flattery, lavished by the score,
Were so much Greek to her and little more.[2]
Wherefore will he devise a stratagem.
Pierre—if I may speak ad hominem—
Was passing dull and none too swift of wit;
Nor ever would presume (as well befit
One of his class) to ask Messire a boon.
The latter though—our would-be cleric lover—
Was glad to offer counsel opportune

L'autre luy dit: compere mon ami
Te voila pauvre, et n'ayant à demi
Ce qu'il te faut; si je t'apprends la guise
Et le moyen d'estre un jour plus contant
Qu'un petit Roy, sans te tourmenter tant,
Que me veux tu donner pour mes estreines?
Pierre répond: Parbleu messire Jean
Je suis à vous; disposez de mes peines;
Car vous sçavez que c'est tout mon vaillant.
Nôtre cochon ne nous faudra pourtant:
Il a mangé plus de son, par mon ame,
Qu'il n'en tiendroit trois fois dans ce tonneau,
Et d'abondant la vache à nôtre femme
Nous a promis qu'elle feroit un veau:
Prenez le tout.—Je ne veux nul salaire,
Dit le Pasteur; obliger mon compere
Ce m'est assez, je te diray comment.
Mon dessein est de rendre Magdeleine
Jument le jour par art d'enchantement;
Luy redonnant sur le soir forme humaine.
Tres-grand profit pourra certainement
T'en revenir; car ton Asne est si lent,
Que du marché l'heure est presque passée
Quand il arrive; ainsi tu ne vends pas,
Comme tu veux, tes herbes, ta denrée,
Tes choux, tes aulx, enfin tout ton tracas.
Ta femme estant jument forte et menbrüe,
Ira plus viste; et si tost que chez toy
Elle sera du marché revenuë,
Sans pain ny soupe un peu d'herbe menuë

(For him himself, that is!). So, one day, soon
Will he arrive. *"Mon cher*, would you discover,"
He asks Pierre, "the means whereby to double
What you possess—or more!—and with less trouble?
Tell me, what will you give me if I show you
How to be rich and happy as a king?"
"Alas, *mon père*, all I possess is woe! You
Know you may take it all! Aye, everything!"
And then, reflecting: "Though, in truth, I do
Have me a pig that I would give to you.
The blessèd beast swills down more feed, I vow,
Than those three barrels full! And my wife's cow...
Aye, aye! I guess that you could take her too.
A fine one, just about to calf." "Now, now,
Dear friend! Nought do I want! Nay, nay!"
Smiles Messire Jean, "save knowing that I may
Oblige my good *compère*. And this is how:
Let me but change your wife into a horse
By day—that is, a proper mare, of course—
By dint of charm and incantation; then
Turn her, by night, to human form again.
Much might you profit from the transformation.
Your ass, alas, is slow of hoof; and when
He hauls your crop you reach your destination
When market day, I fear, is well-nigh done,
And there remains barely a single one
To buy your cabbage, garlic, herbs and such.
Whereas Madame—a rugged, robust mare,
Swift-shanked and lusty-muscled, *au contraire*—
Will take you thereto faster forasmuch.
Once home, think what you save. For all her dinner

Luy suffira. Pierre dit: sur ma foy,
Messire Jean, vous estes un sage homme.
Voyez que c'est d'avoir étudié!
Vend-on cela? si j'avois grosse somme
Je vous l'aurois parbleu bien tost payé.
Jean poursuivit: orça je t'aprendray
Les mots, la guise, et toute la maniere,
Par où jument bien faite et pouliniere
Auras de jour, belle femme de nuit.
Corps, teste, jambe, et tout ce qui s'ensuit
Luy reviendra: tu n'as qu'à me veoir faire.
Tay-toy sur tout; car un mot seulement
Nous gasteroit tout nôtre enchantement.
Nous ne pourrions revenir au mystere,
De nostre vie; encore un coup motus,
Bouche cousüe, ouvre les yeux sans plus:
Toy mesme aprés pratiqueras la chose.
Pierre promet de se taire, et Jean dit:
Sus Magdeleine; il se faut, et pour cause,
Despoüiller nüe et quiter cet habit:
Dégrafez-moy cet atour des Dimanches;
Fort bien: ostez ce corset et ces manches;
Encore mieux: défaites ce jupon;
Tres-bien cela. Quand vint à la chemise,
La pauvre Epouse eut en quelque façon
De la pudeur. Estre nüe ainsi mise
Aux yeux des gens! Magdeleine aymoit mieux
Demeurer femme, et juroit ses grands Dieux
De ne souffrir une telle vergogne.
Pierre luy dit: voilà grande besogne!

She wants no bread, no soup; but, like your ass,
You need shove but some feed or fodder in her,
Or even nothing more, indeed, than grass!"
"Ah," sighs Pierre, "how wise you are! Alas!
Would I had studied too!... This charm... This spell
You speak of... Can I buy it? Do they sell
Such things as these?" The priest replies: "Why spend
Good money? Rather shall I teach you, friend,
What you must say and do, whereby you might
Have sturdy mare by day, stout spouse by night.
As for the rest, *compère*, have no compunction:
Body, head, legs—all will be set to right.
Wife will she be, in form as well as function.
You only have to watch me work. But care!
One word, and all is lost beyond repair:
Spell, mare, adieu! Silence, you understand?
Mouth shut, eyes open, hear? Observe and learn.
See what I do; then you shall too, in turn."
Pierre agrees; and Messire Jean, as planned,
Says to his wife: "Come, Magdeleine. Perforce,
Whoever would, my dear, be made a horse
Needs must, before the deed, get quite undressed.
So off, I pray, with all that Sunday best:
Bauble and bow and fancy frillery!..."
Madame complies... "Fine! Now the corselet...
Ah!... Now the sleeves, trimmed with that filigree...
Good!... Now the petticoat!... Ah! better yet!..."
But when the poor thing reached her chemisette,
Modesty reared its head, and she demurred,
Preferring not to lay her body bare—

Et bien, tous deux nous sçaurons comme quoy
Vous estes faite; est-ce par vostre foy
Dequoy tant craindre? Et là là Magdeleine,
Vous n'avez pas toûjours eu tant de peine
A tout oster: comment donc faites-vous
Quand vous cherchez vos puçes? dites-nous.
Messire Jean est ce quelqu'un d'étrange?
Que craignez-vous? hé quoy? qu'il ne vous mange?
Çà dépeschons; c'est par trop marchandé.
Depuis le temps Monsieur nostre Curé
Auroit des-ja parfait son entreprise.
Disant ces mots il oste la chemise,
Regarde faire, et ses lunettes prend.
Messire Jean par le nombril commençe,
Pose dessus une main en disant:
Que cecy soit beau poitrail de Jument.
Puis cette main dans le pays s'avance.
L'autre s'en va transformer ces deux monts
Qu'en nos climats les gens nomment tetons;
Car quant à ceux qui sur l'autre hemisphere
Sont étendus, plus vastes en leur tour,
Par reverence on ne les nomme guere;
Messire Jean leur fait aussi sa cour;
Disant toûjours pour la ceremonie:
Que cecy soit telle ou telle partie,
Ou belle croupe, ou beaux flancs, tout enfin.
Tant de façons mettoient Pierre en chagrin;
Et ne voyant nul progrés à la chose,
Il prioit Dieu pour la Métamorphose.
C'estoit en vain; car de l'enchantement

Nude, in a word. Whereat objects Pierre:
"Of all the silliest things I ever heard!
You swear—ye gods!—to save your woman's virtue.
But how the Devil is it going to hurt you
To let us look on you? There, there! You never
Made any fuss before—nay, none whatever—
To take off all your clothes! What do you do
To pick your fleas and stop them biting you?
Besides, is Messire Jean a perfect stranger?
What's your objection? What can be the danger?
You think he's going to eat you? Come! Enough!
By now he could have changed you, head to toe."
So saying, he takes her undergarment off;
Puts on his spectacles to watch; and so
Begins the operation. Our *curé*,
Commencing with her navel, lays thereon
An eager, probing hand, and thereupon
Offers his incantation: "Stomach, pray,
Be thou fair, comely belly of a mare."
Whereon the hand wanders the countryside.
The other ventures northward to that pair
Of hillocks, parted by a deep divide,
That, in our climes, go by the name of "tits."
As for their counterparts, round to the rear,
That amply fill the southern hemisphere,
Rather shall I not name them, as befits
A proper awe and veneration; though
Our prelate pays them no less court—oh, no!
So, with much laying on of hands, each part
Will undergo the horse-transformer's art,

Toute la force et l'accomplissement
Gisoit à mettre une queuë à la beste:
Tel ornement est chose fort honneste:
Jean ne voulant un tel poinct oublier
L'attache donc: lors Pierre de crier,
Si haut qu'on l'eust entendu d'une lieuë:
Messire Jean je n'y veux point de queuë:
Vous l'attachez trop bas, Messire Jean.
Pierre à crier ne fut si diligent,
Que bonne part de la ceremonie
Ne fust des-ja par le Prestre accomplie.
A bonne fin le reste auroit esté,
Si non contant d'avoir des-ja parlé
Pierre encor n'eust tiré par la Soutane
Le Curé Jean, qui luy dit: foin, de toy:
T'avois-je pas recommandé, gros asne,
De ne rien dire, et de demeurer coy?
Tout est gasté, ne t'en pren qu'à toy mesme.
Pendant ces mots l'Epoux gronde à part soy.
Magdeleine est en un courroux extreme,
Querelle Pierre, et luy dit: malheureux,
Tu ne seras qu'un miserable gueux
Toute ta vie; et puis vien-t'en me braire;
Vien me conter ta faim et ta douleur.
Voyez un peu: Monsieur nostre Pasteur
Veut de sa grace à ce traisne-malheur
Monstrer dequoy finir nostre misere:
Merite t-il le bien qu'on luy veut faire?
Messire Jean laissons là cet oyson:
Tous les matins tandis que ce veau lie

With many a "Be thou this!" and "Be thou that!"—
Fair rump, fair flanks, fair everything; while poor
Pierre, seeing no change at all thereat,
Prays God to ease his great discomfiture.
To no avail. "Ah," says Messire, "for sure!
The spell, to work, demands a tail!" "Do tell,"
Replies the former, as before his eyes
The latter plants one firmly in the belle.
Whereat: "No tail! No tail!" our husband cries—
Nay, shrieks! "You're putting it too low, *mon père!*"
But still, despite his shouts, rending the air,
Messire—come close to finishing the rite—
Would have discharged his final office, quite
(And all that such entailed), had not Pierre
Tugged at his cassock. "Hellfire and damnation!"
Curses the priest. "Didn't I tell you, lout,
To shut your mouth and not go shouting out!
You've spoiled the spell and stopped the transformation!"³
The husband grumbles as the wife, the while,
Chagrined beyond all telling, roundly chides him;
Calls him all kinds of names; defiles, derides him:
"Oh, what a lowly wretch! Oh, what a vile,
Unholy fool! And ever shall you be!
Well, never come complaining now to me!
Good Messire Jean has finally found a way
To save us from our woe, our misery;
And he, what does he do? Ah, *mon curé,*
Enough of him! But, as for you, each day
I pray you visit, while my Monsieur Fop
Is off attending to his famous crop

Ses choux, ses aulx, ses herbes, son oignon,
Sans l'avertir venez à la maison;
Vous me rendrez une Jument polie.
Pierre reprit: plus de Jument, mamie;
Je suis contant de n'avoir qu'un grison.

Of cabbage, garlic, herbs, and all the rest!
Each morning shall I let you try your best
To turn me to a mare!" Cries husband: "Stop!
No more about that blasted mare, sweet lass!
I'm quite content, my love, with just one ass."

Pierre the Peasant and His Mare

Pasté d'anguille

Mesme beauté, tant soit exquise,
Rassasie, et soûle à la fin.
Il me faut d'un et d'autre pain;
Diversité c'est ma devise.
Cette maîtresse un tantet bize
Rit à mes yeux; pourquoy cela?
C'est qu'elle est neuve; et celle-la
Qui depuis long-temps m'est acquise,
Blanche qu'elle est, en nulle guise
Ne me cause d'émotion.
Son cœur dit ouy; le mien dit non;
D'où vient? en voicy la raison,
Diversité c'est ma devise.
Je l'ay ja-dit d'autre façon;
Car il est bon que l'on desguise
Suivant la Loy de ce dicton,
Diversité c'est ma devise.
Ce fut celle aussi d'un mary
De qui la femme estoit fort belle.
Il se trouva bien tost guery
De l'amour qu'il avoit pour elle.
L'Hymen, et la possession
Eteignirent sa passion.
Un sien Valet avoit pour femme
Un petit bec assez mignon:
Le maistre estant bon compagnon,
Eut bien tost empaumé la Dame.
Cela ne plût pas au Valet,
Qui les ayant pris sur le fait,

The Eel Pâté

Time mutes our pleasures, dulls our joys.
However exquisite it be,
Even a lady's beauty cloys:
My motto is "Diversity."
So is it with the bread I eat:
If rye today, tomorrow wheat.
This mistress seems a trifle tan,
Yet pleasures me. You ask me: "Why?
Explain your taste." And well I can.
She's new, you see; whilst she whom I
Have had the while is fair of skin,
But I take little joy therein.
My heart says "*Non!*" though hers sighs "*Oui!*"—
My motto is "Diversity."
(This have I said in other wise.
But such a thought I ought disguise
In divers ways, you must agree:
My motto is "Diversity"!)
So too was it the motto of
The husband of a beauteous belle,
Who found himself soon cured of love.
For wedlock and the rights thereof
Are quick indeed to cool—nay, quell—
Man's passion, as they did with his.
The husband has a man, who is,
In turn, the husband of a sprightly,
Pert, comely *demoiselle*. Now then,
The master—not some Jack-go-lightly,
And quite the heartiest of men—

Vendiqua son bien de couchete,
A sa moitié chanta goguette,
L'appella tout net et tout franc…
Bien sot de faire un bruit si grand
Pour une chose si commune;
Dieu nous gard de plus grand fortune.
Il fit à son Maistre un sermon.
Monsieur, dit-il, chacun la sienne
Ce n'est pas trop; Dieu et raison
Vous recommandent cétte Antienne.
Direz-vous, je suis sans Chrestienne?
Vous en avez à la maison
Une qui vaut cent fois la mienne.
Ne prenez donc plus tant de peine:
C'est pour ma femme trop d'honneur;
Il ne lui faut si gros Monsieur.
Tenons-nous chacun à la nostre;
N'allez point à l'eau chez un autre,
Ayant plein puits de ces douceurs;
Je m'en raporte aux connoisseurs:
Si Dieu m'avoit fait tant de grace,
Qu'ainsi que vous je disposasse
De Madame, je m'y tiendrois,
Et d'une Reine ne voudrois.
Mais puis qu'on ne sçauroit défaire
Ce qui s'est fait, je voudrois bien,
(Ceci soit dit sans vous deplaire,)
Que contant de vostre ordinaire
Vous ne goûtassiez plus du mien.
Le Patron ne voulut luy dire
Ni oüy ny non sur ce discours;

Promptly seduced the wife (by hook
And crook!); whereat his minion took
Much umbrage, catching them, in fact,
In bed; yea, in the very act.
One look, and he, as it behooved him,
Railed at his mate; accused, attacked
With oath and curse. But she reproved him,
Saying that she was loath to see
Why such a common thing so moved him;
That he was surely daft to be
So vexed; and "please God, may we never
Know any worse woe whatsoever!"
He chides his master too; makes free
With sermon, courteous but direct:
"God and good reason, sire, decree
That I, and—saving your respect—
That you, have but one wife alone:
One wife for each; to each his own.
What? Will you say that you have none
When you, forsooth, have such a one,
Worth more than mine a hundredfold?
Much too much honor do you do
My humble spouse: *merci beaucoup!*
But sire, if I may be so bold,
She needs no gentle squire so fine:
You keep to yours; I'll keep to mine.
Your well is full of sweets untold:
No cause to dip your pipkin, please,
In mine when yours has ones like these.
If God had granted me the bliss
To use Madame as I so choose,
Even a queen would I refuse!

Et commanda que tous les jours
On mist aux repas, prés du sire,
Un pasté d'Anguille; ce mets
Luy chatoüilloit fort le palais.
Avec un appetit extreme
Une et deux fois il en mangea:
Mais quand ce vint à la troisiesme
La seule odeur le dégoûta.
Il voulut sur une autre viande
Mettre la main; on l'empêcha:
Monsieur, dit-on, nous le commande:
Tenez-vous en à ce mets-là:
Vous l'aimez, qu'avez-vous à dire?
—M'en voila soû, reprit le Sire.
Et quoy toûjours pastez au bec!
Pas une Anguille de rostie!
Pastez tous les jours de ma vie!
J'aymerois-mieux du pain tout sec:
Laissez-moy prendre un peu du vôtre:
Pain de par Dieu, ou de par l'autre:
Au Diable ces pastez maudits;
Ils me suivront en Paradis,
Et par delà, Dieu me pardonne.
Le Maistre accourt soudain au bruit,
Et prenant sa part du deduit,
Mon Amy, dit-il, je m'étonne
Que d'un mets si plein de bonté
Vous soyez si tôt dégoûté.
Ne vous ay-je pas ouy dire
Que c'estoit vôtre grand ragoût?
Il faut qu'en peu de temps, beau Sire,

Ah well, what's done is done. But this
Is all I have to say, monsieur:
My wife cannot undo, indeed,
The dalliance that you did with her.
Yet would I ask you, sire, to heed
My earnest prayer: be satisfied
With yours and leave my own to me."
The master neither "Aye" replied
Nor "Nay." But now, summarily,
He asks that every meal, each day,
His man be served an eel pâté—
His favorite savory, truth to tell.
First day, then second: sheer delight!
But by the third, the very smell
Of eel pâté disgusts him, quite.
He yearns for something else... Resists...
Requests... But no! "Monsieur insists,"
They say. So, every day and night,
More eel pâté; less appetite...
"At least," cried he, "why can't they make it
Some other way? Sauté it... Bake it...
But why pâté, pâté, pâté?
I'd rather one dry crust, I pray...
God's bread or Satan's? Fine! I'll take it!
Anything but this tiresome fare:
These loathesome, damned pâtés! I swear,
They'd follow me to heaven above me,
And farther if they could, God love me!"
The master, when he hears the noise,
Comes running in and much enjoys
His minion's great discomfiture.

Vous ayez bien changé de goût?
Qu'ay-je fait qui fust plus étrange?
Vous me blâmez lors que je change
Un mets que vous croyez friand,
Et vous en faites tout autant.
Mon doux Amy, je vous aprend
Que ce n'est pas une sottise,
En fait de certains apetits,
De changer son pain blanc en bis:
Diversité c'est ma Devise.
Quand le Maistre eut ainsi parlé,
Le Valet fut tout consolé.
Non que ce dernier n'eust à dire
Quelque chose encor la dessus:
Car aprés tout doit-il suffire
D'alléguer son plaisir sans plus?
—J'ayme le change.—A la bonne heure,
On vous l'accorde; mais gagnez
S'il se peut les interessez:
Cette voye est bien la meilleure:
Suivez-la donc. A dire vray,
Je crois que l'Amateur du change
De ce Conseil tenta l'essay.
On dit qu'il parloit comme un Ange,
De mots dorez usant toûjours:
Mots dorez font tout en Amours.
C'est une maxime constante:
Chacun sçait quelle est mon entente:
J'ai rebatu cent et cent fois
Cecy dans cent et cent endroits:
Mais la chose est si necessaire,

"My friend," says he, "I thought for sure
That you could have no fonder wish
Than to consume this dainty dish—
If I recall, your favorite.
Now—O surprise!—you curse my fish
And utter cries of scorn for it.
In but a trice, you must admit,
Your taste has turned. You may surmise,
Likewise has mine. So pray refrain
From scolding me when I disdain
A dish you deem I ought to prize.
No folly is it, friend, nor strange,
When, to our taste, perchance, we change
Dark breads for light, or wheats for ryes:
My motto is 'Diversity.' "
Minion, consoled to great degree
By master's apt analogy,[1]
Has, nonetheless, a reservation.
For, after all, should pleasure be
His one and only compensation?
"I thrive on change." So be it: thrive.
But minions, to be well consoled,
Are better served with words of gold.
The master did, indeed, contrive
To speak with golden voice. We're told
That he spoke like an angel; just
As rich, aspiring lovers must.
For "gilded words speak loud in love."
You must have heard that saw before:
Hundreds of times from me, and more!
Beside, behind, below, above—
Everywhere is this maxim spoken.

Que je ne puis jamais m'en taire,
Et rediray jusques au bout,
Mots dorez en Amours font tout.
Ils persuadent la Donzelle,
Son petit chien, sa Demoiselle,
Son Epoux quelque fois aussi;
C'est le seul qu'il falloit icy
Persuader; il n'avoit l'ame
Sourde à cette eloquence; et Dame
Les Orateurs du temps jadis
N'en ont de telle en leurs écrits.
Nôtre jaloux devint commode.
Même on dit qu'il suivit la mode
De son Maistre, et toûjours depuis
Changea d'objets en ses deduits.
Il n'estoit bruit que d'avantures
Du Chrétien et de Creatures.
Les plus nouvelles sans manquer
Estoient pour luy les plus gentilles.
Par où le drôle en pût croquer,
Il en croqua, femmes et filles,
Nimphes, Grisettes, ce qu'il put.
Toutes estoient de bonne prise;
Et sur ce poinct, tant qu'il vescut,
Diversité fut sa Devise.

But let the reader, tired thereof,
Yet not suppose that, by that token,
I shall desist, chastised and cowed,
From saying, as often as I would,
That "gilded words, in love, speak loud."
"What use are they?" you ask. "What good?"
Just this: their jingling sounds persuade
The lady fair; her dog;[2] her maid;
And sometimes husband too, as here
(The most important of the lot!).
Ours hears their message, loud and clear:
Jealous before; now, not a jot!
Fairer than bards' fair belles of old,
Wife falls before those words of gold.
What's more, our minion—so they tell us—
Not only ceases to be jealous,
But learns the master's sport. Behold!
See how he flits from wife, to lass,
To wench, to nymph... She flees? He'll get her!—
The younger and less used the better—
Until, in brief, what comes to pass?
The country round hums, all a-buzz,
With what this randy rascal does.
No more the steadfast husband, he:
His motto now: "Diversity!"

Les Lunettes

J'avois juré de laisser là les Nones:
Car que toûjours on voye en mes écrits
Mesme sujet, et semblables personnes,
Cela pourroit fatiguer les esprits.
Ma muse met Guimpe sur le tapis:
Et puis quoy? Guimpe; et puis Guimpe sans cesse;
Bref toûjours Guimpe, et Guimpe sous la presse.
C'est un peu trop. Je veux que les Nonains
Fassent les tours en amour les plus fins;
Si ne faut-il pour cela qu'on épuise
Tout le sujet; le moyen? c'est un fait
Par trop fréquent, je n'aurois jamais fait:
Il n'est Greffier dont la plume y suffise.
Si j'y tâchois on pourroit soupçonner
Que quelque cas m'y feroit retourner;
Tant sur ce poinct mes Vers font de rechutes;
Toûjours souvient à Robin de ses flûtes.
Or apportons à cela quelque fin.
Je le prétends, cette tâche icy faite.
Jadis s'estoit introduit un blondin
Chez des Nonains à titre de fillette.
Il n'avoit pas quinze ans que tout ne fust:
Dont le galant passa pour sœur Colette
Auparavant que la barbe luy crust.
Cet entre temps ne fut sans fruit; le Sire
L'employa bien: Agnés en profita.
Las quel profit! j'eusse mieux fait de dire
Qu'à sœur Agnés malheur en arriva.
Il luy falut élargir sa ceinture;

The Spectacles

Not long ago, you may recall, I swore
To leave the nuns alone and tweak no more
Their habits.[1] For, perforce, if I rehearse
Ever the same refrain; if, in my verse,
The same folk keep appearing as before,
Soon will my reader tire. Now, though the veil
Amuses much my Muse, I should abuse her
By overuse, and would not so misuse her.
Little would it avail if every tale
Twitted the veil: veil now and veil anon.
So let the blessèd sisters carry on
With canny wiles and amorous artifices.
Who can exhaust a subject such as this is?
No scribe who might attempt to write thereon
Would have, I think, sufficient ink to do it.
Myself, though I should promise to eschew it,
I daresay I could always find a story
Of nun undone by venture amatory.
Robin, forsooth, however resolute,
Can never quite refuse to play his flute![2]
Still will I try. But first, one tale: in truth,
My last about the veil!... A certain youth
There was: a tender lad of fifteen years—
At most—who, not yet dry behind the ears,
So much appeared a virgin maid that he
Was able to invade a nunnery
And live amongst the nuns as Sœur Colette.
Smooth-skinned and beardless, our inferred *nymphette*
Put to good use that youthful callowness.
In time it was the gentle Sœur Agnès

Puis mettre au jour petite creature,
Qui ressembloit comme deux goutes d'eau,
Ce dit l'histoire, à la sœur Jouvenceau.
Voila scandale et bruit dans l'Abbaye.
D'où cet enfant est-il plu? comme a-t-on,
Disoient les sœurs en riant, je vous prie,
Trouvé çeans çe petit champignon?
Si ne s'est-il aprés tout fait luy mesme.
La Prieure est en un courroux extreme.
Avoir ainsi soüillé cette maison!
Bien tost on mit l'accouchée en prison.
Puis il falut faire enqueste du pere.
Comment est-il entré? comment sorti?
Les murs sont hauts, antique la touriere,
Double la grille, et le tour tres petit.
Seroit ce point quelque garçon en fille?
Dit la Prieure, et parmi nos brebis
N'aurions nous point sous de trompeurs habits
Un jeune loup? sus qu'on se des-habille:
Je veux sçavoir la verité du cas.
Qui fut bien pris, ce fut la feinte oüaille.
Plus son esprit à songer se travaille,
Moins il espere échaper d'un tel pas.
Necessité mere de stratagême
Luy fit... eh bien? luy fit en ce moment
Lier...: eh quoy? foin, je suis court moy-mesme:
Où prendre un mot qui dise honnestement
Ce que lia le pere de l'enfant?
Comment trouver un détour suffisant
Pour cet endroit? Vous avez oüi dire
Qu'au temps jadis le genre humain avoit

Who profited therefrom. "Profited" did I say?
Rather would "suffered" be a better word.
For she soon found her belt—ah, welladay!—
Becoming, more and more, too tight to gird
Her belly; felt it swelling, till she bore
A babe unbidden and unbargained for,
Looking for all the world (or so I've heard)
Like so-called Sœur Colette. Now, surely you
Can well imagine what occurred. A-twitter,
The nuns—with many a laugh, all chaff and titter—
Discuss the "why," the "when," the "how," the "who":
"What? Fallen from the clouds?" "Indeed!" "No doubt!"
"Or did it just, I wonder, up and sprout
After the rain, the way some mushrooms do?"
As for the prioress, you must have guessed
That she was most dismayed and much distressed.
"O scandal! O disgrace!" she cried. And she
Had Sœur Agnès put under lock and key.
Whereat the Reverend Mother did her best
To find the father: how it came that he
Entered thereto and left so easily.
"High are our walls... Two gates, and stout the locks...
And sister who attends the turning-box—
Who minds the goings-out and comings-in—
Is much too old to tempt, and long has been
A faithful servant... Could it be, I wonder,
Some male in maiden's guise, and hidden under
The falsest of pretense? Wolf garbed herein
In sheep's attire," she muses, "bent on plunder?
Well, we'll soon see!" And she commands: "Undress!
Now shall I give the matter my attention."

Fenestre au corps; de sorte qu'on pouvoit
Dans le dedans tout à son aise lire;
Chose commode aux Medecins d'alors.
Mais si d'avoir une fenestre au corps
Estoit utile, une au cœur au contraire
Ne l'estoit pas; dans les femmes sur tout:
Car le moyen qu'on pust venir à bout
De rien cacher? Nostre commune mere
Dame Nature y pourveut sagement
Par deux lacets de pareille mesure.
L'homme et la femme eurent également
Dequoy fermer une telle ouverture.
La femme fut laçée un peu trop dru.
Ce fut sa faute, elle mesme en fut cause;
N'estant jamais à son gré trop bien close.
L'homme au rebours; et le bout du tissu
Rendit en luy la nature perplexe.
Bref le laçet à l'un et l'autre sexe
Ne put quadrer, et se trouva, dit-on,
Aux femmes court, aux hommes un peu long.
Il est facile à présent qu'on devine
Ce que lia nostre jeune imprudent;
C'est ce surplus, ce reste de machine,
Bout de laçet aux hommes excedant.
D'un brin de fil il l'attacha de sorte
Que tout sembloit aussi plat qu'aux Nonains:
Mais fil ou soye, il n'est bride assez forte
Pour contenir ce que bientost je crains
Qui ne s'échape; amenez moy des saints;
Amenez-moy si vous voulez des Anges;
Je les tiendray creatures estranges,

Young sire knew all was lost, alas, unless
Necessity, that mother of invention,
Inspired him with a stratagem. She did.
What did he do? He tied... He bound... He hid
His... his... How shall I put it? That is... Damn!
It isn't often, poet that I am,
That I'm caught at a loss for words. But how
Shall I, in decent wise, say what our sham
Colette bound up betwixt his thighs?... Well now,
Who tries succeeds. I'll try the best I can.[3]
The Ancients used to say that early Man
Sported a lengthy hole that would allow
The doctors of that bygone day to tell
With ease whatever harm or ill befell
Their patients. But, though useful for their art,
This window, so to speak, undid the heart.
Woman's especially. For how could she
Keep secret what she wanted none to see?
And so it was that Mother Nature found
The way to lace it shut, quite properly.
But man, content to be less tightly bound
Than woman—ever firmly corseted!—
Used up less lacing and, so is it said,
Nonplussed poor Nature with his long excess...
There! Now I trust my meaning is revealed
Clearly enough to let the reader guess
Just what it was our rash young swain concealed.
He tied it down, pulled back so flat that one
Would not have known Monsieur was not a nun.
But thread nor twine, however stout and strong—
Even the finest silk—cannot, for long,
Restrain said object once it has begun

Si vingt Nonains telles qu'on les vid lors
Ne font trouver à leur esprit un corps.
J'entends Nonains ayant tous les tresors
De ces trois sœurs dont la fille de l'onde
Se fait servir; chiches et fiers appas,
Que le soleil ne void qu'au nouveau monde,
Car celuy-cy ne les luy monstre pas.
La Prieure a sur son nez des lunettes,
Pour ne juger du cas legerement.
Tout à l'entour sont debout vingt Nonettes,
En un habit que vray-semblablement
N'avoient pas fait les tailleurs du Couvent.
Figurez-vous la question qu'au Sire
On donna lors; besoin n'est de le dire.
Touffes de lis, proportion du corps,
Secrets appas, enbonpoinct, et peau fine,
Fermes tetons, et semblables ressorts
Eurent bien tost fait joüer la machine.
Elle eschapa, rompit le fil d'un coup,
Comme un coursier qui romproit son licou,
Et sauta droit au nez de la Prieure,
Faisant voler lunettes tout à l'heure
Jusqu'au plancher. Il s'en falut bien peu
Que l'on ne vist tomber la lunetiere.
Elle ne prit cet accident en jeu.
L'on tint Chapitre, et sur cette matiere
Fut raisonné long-temps dans le logis.
Le jeune loup fut aux vieilles brebis
Livré d'abord. Elles vous l'empoignerent,
A certain arbre en leur cour l'attacherent,
Ayant le nez devers l'arbre tourné,

To chafe against its bridle! No constraints
Can hold that excess down. Bring me your saints,
Your angels! One must be a prodigy
To look, unmoved, on maids whose unclad beauty
Rivals the Graces', Venus's minions three.
(Charms that the New World sees far more than we!)
The prioress prepares to do her duty,
Spectacles perched on nose, attentively.
About her stand some twenty nymph nunnettes,
Garbed in their birthday habits—unprotected—
Garments no convent seamsters have confected!
You know the shocked surprise his state begets
When comes the time our lad must be inspected.
Soon secret pleasures—treasures—meet his eye:
Firm, full-formed bodies, lily-tufted flesh,
Nipples erect, skin soft and smooth and fresh...
Ah! But an instant and, as he stands by,
Suddenly liberated from its prison,
His said device, bonds broken, springs arisen
Like steed that snaps its halter, bounding free;
And sends the holy mother's glasses flying
Into the air, unceremoniously—
Needless, indeed, to say, quite horrifying
Our pious *mère*, bespectacled no more—
And almost knocks her to the convent floor.
The prioress was not amused, nor took
The matter lightly. Should the sisters brook
Such infamy? The chapter was convened
To wreak revenge upon their wolfish fiend.
After much long, detailed deliberation,
Unto the elder lambs its wrath consigned him.

Le dos à l'air avec toute la suite:
Et cependant que la troupe maudite
Songe comment il sera guerdonné,
Que l'une va prendre dans les Cuisines
Tous les balays, et que l'autre s'en court
A l'Arsenal où sont les disciplines,
Qu'une troisiesme enferme à double tour
Les Sœurs qui sont jeunes et pitoyables,
Bref que le sort ami du marjeolet
Ecarte ainsi toutes les détestables,
Vient un Meusnier monté sur son mulet,
Garçon quarré, garçon couru des filles,
Bon Compagnon, et beau joüeur de quilles.
Oh oh dit-il, qu'est-ce là que je voy?
Le plaisant saint! jeune homme, je te prie,
Qui t'a mis là? sont-ce ces sœurs, dis-moy.
Avec quelqu'une as tu fait la folie?
Te plaisoit elle? estoit-elle jolie?
Car à te voir tu me portes ma foy
(Plus je regarde et mire ta personne)
Tout le minois d'un vray croqueur de None.
L'autre répond: helas, c'est le rebours:
Ces Nones m'ont en vain prié d'amours.
Voila mon mal; Dieu me doint patience;
Car de commettre une si grande offence,
J'en fais scrupule, et fust-ce pour le Roy;
Me donnast-on aussi gros d'or que moy.
Le Meusnier rit; et sans autre mystere
Vous le délie, et luy dit: idiot,
Scrupule toy, qui n'es qu'un pauvre haire!
C'est bien à nous qu'il appartient d'en faire!

They lead him to a tree, and there they bind him
(Nose toward the trunk, for fittest expiation:
Behind perforce before); prance round behind him;
Subject him to their vengeful contemplation:
How best to give him tit for tat (and tat
For tit, forsooth: eye, tooth, and all of that).
Some go to fetch their brooms; some run and get
Their scourges; yet some others take the trouble
To lock the young nuns' doors—and lock them double!—
To keep each tender-hearted *mignonnette*
Pent in her cell. Thus does a kindly fate
Smile on our now unguarded reprobate.
Just then, a miller on his ass lopes by
(Stout, fit: a much-sought beau, but pleasant chap
All things considered); gives the youth the eye.
"Oh, oh! What's this I see? I'd say, mayhap,
A certain sorry saint made much too free
With some young lovely in the nunnery!
Tell me, what was she like? A pretty one?
To look at you, I'm sure you must, monsieur—
Much as you will—get quite your fill of nun!"
"Ah, to the contrary, my friend: you err,"
Replies the other, "True, those nuns desire me,
And would, by force, prevail. Yet I prefer
To turn my back. For, much though they inspire me
With love and lust, I must—God grant!—resist.
Not for my weight in gold; not for the king
Himself would I do such a wicked thing!"
Chortles the miller: "Well, if you insist,
Imbecile! 'Wicked thing!...' Why shouldn't you,
Poor wretch, do what our good *curé* will do?

Nostre Curé ne seroit pas si sot.
Viste, fuy-t'en, m'ayant mis en ta plaçe:
Car aussi bien tu n'es pas comme moy
Franc du collier, et bon pour cet employ:
Je n'y veux point de quartier ny de grace:
Viennent ces sœurs; toutes je te répon
Verront beau jeu si la corde ne rompt.
L'autre deux fois ne se le fait redire.
Il vous l'attache, et puis luy dit adieu.
Large d'épaule on auroit veu le Sire
Attendre nud les Nonains en ce lieu.
L'escadron vient, porte en guise de Cierges
Gaules et foüets: procession de verges
Qui fit la ronde à l'entour du Meusnier,
Sans luy donner le temps de se montrer,
Sans l'avertir. Tout beau, dit-il, mes Dames:
Vous vous trompez; considerez-moy bien:
Je ne suis pas cet ennemi des femmes,
Ce scrupuleux qui ne vaut rien à rien.
Emploiez moy, vous verrez des merveilles.
Si je dis faux, coupez moy les oreilles.
D'un certain jeu je viendray bien à bout;
Mais quant au foüet je n'y vaux rien du tout.
—Qu'entend ce Rustre, et que nous veut il dire,
S'écria lors une de nos sans-dents.
Quoy tu n'es pas nostre faiseur d'enfans?
Tant pis pour toy, tu payras pour le sire.
Nous n'avons pas telles armes en main,
Pour demeurer en un si beau chemin.
Tien tien, voila l'ébat que l'on desire.
A ce discours foüets de rentrer en jeu,

Who better than the likes of you and me
For such a task?... And me especially,
Strong and well suited to the saddle!... Here!
I'll take your place... Be quick! Be off!... They'll see,
I ask no quarter! Let those nuns appear:
They'll need no cords to hold me, never fear!"
Only too ready now to acquiesce,
Happily freed, our beau agreed; and, tying
His saviour to the tree, off he went flying,
Leaving the miller in his nakedness—
Back broad and bare—to stand there, waiting.
Comes the parade of vestals, celebrating
Now not with candles but with switch and scourge,
Defiling undefiled, gesticulating...⁴
With never a glance they congregate, converge,
Surround the miller, still without a stitch,
About to whip and pummel him. At which:
"*Mes sœurs!*" he cries. "Wait! Look! I'm not the one
You think. That prude! That worthless woman-hater!
Use me to do your will: your will be done!
And well, believe me," promises our prater.
"I'll do you all! And you'll be done as none
Has ever done you! If I lie, I'll let you
Cut off my ears! But sticks and whips will get you
Nothing, I vow, that you'll not get without them."
Hearing his words and wondering about them:
"What is this bumpkin babbling?" cries a crone,
One of the toothless troop, well-worn and haggard.
"What? Are you not that baby-making blackguard?
Well, friend, *tant pis!* No less shall you atone
For him! We've not come armed for nought, I own!"

Verges d'aller, et non pas pour un peu;
Meusnier de dire en langue intelligible,
Crainte de n'estre assez bien entendu,
Mes Dames je... feray tout mon possible
Pour m'acquiter de ce qui vous est dû.
Plus il leur tient des discours de la sorte,
Plus la fureur de l'antique cohorte
Se fait sentir. Long-temps il s'en souvint.
Pendant qu'on donne au Maistre l'anguillade,
Le mulet fait sur l'herbette gambade.
Ce qu'à la fin l'un et l'autre devint,
Je ne le sçais, ny ne m'en mets en peine.
Suffit d'avoir sauvé le jouvenceau.
Pendant un temps les lecteurs pour douzaine
De ces Nonains au corps gent et si beau
N'auroient voulu, je gage, être en sa peau.

With which, she and the others rain their blows:
Whips, switches, scourges, sticks... And so it goes.
"But," reaffirms the miller, fearing he
Has not been understood sufficiently,
"Mesdames, I told you I would gladly do
What—and whom—ever you desire me to. 5
Really, you needn't use such force on me!"
The more he spoke, the more they whipped. His ass,
The while, sported and gamboled on the grass.
Master and beast... What happened then? *Qui sait?*
I neither know nor care. And, anyway,
What matters most is that we saved the youth.
Still, for a dozen of those nuns, forsooth—
The comely ones!—my readers would not choose
To spend much time, I warrant, in his shoes.

The Spectacles

Le Cuvier

Soiez Amant, vous serez inventif:
Tour ny détour, ruse ny stratageme
Ne vous faudront: le plus jeune aprentif
Est vieux routier des le moment qu'il aime:
On ne vit onc que cette passion
Demeurast court faute d'invention:
Amour fait tant qu'enfin il a son conte.
Certain Cuvier, dont on fait certain conte,
En fera foy. Voicy ce que j'en sçais,
Et qu'un quidam me dit ces jours passés.
Dedans un bourg ou ville de Province,
(N'importe pas du titre ny du nom)
Un Tonnelier et sa femme Nanon
Entretenoient un mesnage assez minçe.
De l'aller voir amour n'eut à mépris;
Y conduisant un de ses bons amis;
C'est cocüage; il fut de la partie;
Dieux familiers, et sans ceremonie,
Se trouvans bien dans toute hostellerie;
Tout est pour eux bon giste et bon logis;
Sans regarder si c'est louvre ou cabane.
Un drosle donc caressoit Madame Anne.
Ils en estoient sur un poinct, sur un poinct...
C'est dire assez de ne le dire point,
Lors que l'Espoux revient tout hors d'haleine
Du Cabaret; justement, justement...
C'est dire encor ceci bien clairement.
On le maudit; nos gens sont fort en peine.
Tout ce qu'on put, fut de cacher l'Amant:

The Tub

Would you be clever? Well then, be a lover.
Artifice, ruse, wile, artful stratagem—
Even Love's youngest greenhorns will discover
How to be practiced veterans with them.
For, witless Love is not—nay, not a whit—
But rather thrives the more through use of it.
A certain tale about a certain tub
Someone just told me proves my case. To wit:
In country town—or village (what we dub
The place makes little difference to my story)—
A cooper lived, in manner desultory,
With wife Nanon. But—aye, and here's the rub—
Betwixt the two there dwelt as well, not Love,
But one that he's a boon companion of:
That other household god named Cuckoldry.
(Like Love, he lives offhand and *en famille*,
Round and about: fine palace,¹ lowly sty,
Or cooper's house, indeed...) Now, by the by,
Nanon was with her lover making free
One day—and he with her no less, need I
Aver?—when both were just about... about...
(No call, I think, to spell that sentence out.)
Yes, as they're in the act... there in the act...
(And even clearer, that!) Well, then and there,
Who should come running up, with breathless air,
Back from the tavern, but monsieur, in fact!
The pair—cursing, despairing—run outside
To where the hogsheads, casks, and kegs are stacked,
And barely have just time enough to hide
The beau inside one of the tubs, inverted.

On vous le serre en haste et promptement
Sous un cuvier, dans une cour prochaine.
Tout en entrant l'Espoux dit: j'ay vendu
Nostre Cuvier.—Combien? dit Madame Anne.
—Quinze beaux francs.—Va tu n'es qu'un gros Asne,
Repartit elle: et je t'ay d'un escu
Fait aujourd'huy profit par mon adresse,
L'ayant vendu six écus avant toy.
Le Marchand voit s'il est de bon alloy,
Et par dedans le taste pieçe à pieçe,
Examinant si tout est comme il faut,
Si quelque endroit n'a point quelque defaut.
Que ferois tu malheureux sans ta femme?
Monsieur s'en va chopiner, cependant
Qu'on se tourmente icy le corps et l'ame:
Il faut agir sans cesse en l'attendant.
Je n'ay gousté jusqu'icy nulle joye:
J'en gousteray desormais, atten t'y.
Voyez un peu, le galand a bon foye:
Je suis d'avis qu'on laisse à tel mary
Telle moitié.—Doucement nostre Espouse,
Dit le bonhomme. Or sus Monsieur, sortés
Çà que je racle un peu de tous costés
Vostre Cuvier, et puis que je l'arrouse.
Par ce moyen vous verrez s'il tient eau,
Je vous réponds qu'il n'est moins bon que beau.
Le galant sort; l'époux entre en sa place,
Racle par tout, la chandelle à la main,
Deçà delà, sans qu'il se doute brin
De ce qu'amour en dehors vous luy brasse:
Rien n'en put voir; et pendant qu'il repasse

"Nanon! Nanon! Good news!" the cooper blurted.
"That tub of ours... I've sold it!" "Oh?" she cried,
Approaching. "And how much?" "Full fifteen francs."
"Fifteen...? Five crown? You stupid twit! No thanks!
I sold that very tub just now for six.
But for my skill you would have lost one crown.
See? Even now the buyer pokes and kicks
About inside[2]—here, there, and up and down—
To give the tub his carefulest inspection
Lest he detect some flaw or imperfection.
What would you do without your wife, poor ass!
But no! Monsieur goes tippling at the inn.
Others he leaves to toil and moil herein,
Till his good pleasure brings him home, alas!
Pleasure? How much have I? Nought but chagrin!
Well, pleasure shall I have, believe you me!"
The husband swallows what the wife serves up.[3]
(Such wives as thrive on mates' credulity—
The more they dish, the more their men will sup.)
"Now, there now, woman..." tuts the barrelsmith;
And, drawing near the lover's cache, therewith:
"Come out, monsieur," says he, "and let me do
A proper testing of your tub for you.
Why, even will I water it as well,
So that, thereby, you may be quick to tell
How tight it holds. For, ah! my friend," he sighed,
"This is a work no less of craft than beauty!"
The lover leaves; the husband crawls inside,
Candle in hand; performs the cooper's duty,
Rubbing and scrubbing here and there; and never
Aware of what goes on outside, however.

Sur chaque endroit, affublé du cuveau,
Les Dieux susdits luy viennent de nouveau
Rendre visite, imposant un ouvrage
A nos Amans bien different du sien.
Il regrata, grata, frota si bien,
Que nôtre couple, ayant repris courage,
Reprit aussi le fil de l'entretien
Qu'avoit troublé le galant personnage.
Dire comment le tout se put passer,
Amy Lecteur tu dois m'en dispenser:
Suffit que j'ay tres bien prouvé ma these.
Ce tour fripon du couple augmentoit l'aise.
Nul d'eux n'estoit à tels jeux aprentif.
Soyez Amant, vous serez inventif.

For as he pokes and probes his way about,
Checking, within, each stave and joint; without,
Our lovers, lying on the tub, above,
Votaries still of Cuckoldry and Love,
Continue to enjoy that gentle sport
That his unwelcome coming had cut short.
Forgive me, gentle reader, if I fail
To add hereto a lengthy exegesis
Or to relate each intimate detail—
Save that they use their ruse to good avail.
I think I've proved sufficiently my thesis.
No greenhorns they! Nought have they to discover!
Would you be clever? Well then, be a lover.

The Tub

La Chose impossible

Un demon plus noir que malin,
    Fit un charme si souverain
    Pour l'Amant de certaine belle,
Qu'à la fin celuy cy posseda sa cruelle.
Le pact de nostre Amant et de l'esprit folet
Ce fut que le premier joüiroit à souhait
    De sa charmante inexorable.
Je te la rends dans peu, dit Satan, favorable:
Mais par tel si, qu'au lieu qu'on obeit au Diable,
    Quand il a fait ce plaisir là,
A tes commandemens le Diable obeira,
    Sur l'heure mesme, et puis sur la mesme heure
Ton serviteur Lutin, sans plus longue demeure,
Ira te demander autre commandement,
    Que tu luy feras promptement;
Toûjours ainsi, sans nul retardement:
    Sinon, ny ton corps ny ton ame
    N'appartiendront plus à ta Dame;
Ils seront à satan, et satan en fera
    Tout ce que bon lui semblera.
    Le Galand s'accorde à cela.
    Commander, estoit-ce un mystere?
    Obeïr est bien autre affaire.
    Sur ce penser là nostre Amant
S'en va trouver sa belle; en a contentement;
Gouste des voluptez qui n'ont point de pareilles;
Se trouve tres heureux; hormis qu'incessamment
    Le Diable estoit à ses oreilles.
    Alors l'Amant luy commandoit

The Impossible Task

A demon was there, black as pitch,
　But not so fell as might be thought,
Who wrought, for certain beau, a spell by which
He got the willful wench he lately sought.
Most curious was the pact betwixt the twain:
"She shall be yours," Satan had told the swain,
　"Her obstinacy notwithstanding,
Provided you reward my minion—who
　Performs this devilish boon for you—
Rather than by obeying, by commanding.
Your every bidding shall, without ado,
Be done. Then shall your servant-imp come ask
That you oblige him with another task,
　The which you must give instantly.
　Then more and more; and each must be
　Given your sprite no less *instanter*.
For, should you lag," explained the dark enchanter,
"Our compact states that you herewith agree
That forthwith finished is your amorous banter,
And soul and body shall belong to me,
No longer to your lady. Understood?"
　The beau agreed. Indeed, he would
Abide by the conditions thus propounded.
Command? Why not? Better than to obey!
　So off he went—nay, fairly bounded—
To his *inamorata*'s side, surrounded
　By joys unmatched that, night and day,
Resounded to love's rapturous roundelay.
Ecstatic would he be were he not hounded,
Dogged by his demon, ever at his ear,

Tout ce qui lui venoit en teste;
De bâtir des Palais, d'exciter la tempeste;
En moins d'un tour de main cela s'accomplissoit.
    Mainte pistolle se glissoit
    Dans l'escarcelle de nostre homme.
    Il envoioit le Diable à Rome;
Le Diable revenoit tout chargé de pardons.
    Aucuns voyages n'estoient longs,
    Aucune chose malaisée.
    L'Amant à force de rêver
Sur les ordres nouveaux qu'il lui faloit trouver,
    Vid bien-tost sa cervelle usee.
   Il s'en plaignit à sa divinité:
Lui dit de bout en bout toute la verité.
Quoy ce n'est que cela? lui repartit la Dame:
    Je vous auray bien-tost tiré
    Une telle épine de l'ame.
Quand le Diable viendra, vous lui presenterez
    Ce que je tiens, et lui direz:
Défrize-moy cecy; fais tant par tes journées
Qu'il devienne tout plat. Lors elle lui donna
    Je ne sçais quoy qu'elle tira
Du verger de Cypris, labirinte des fées,
Ce qu'un Duc autrefois jugea si precieux,
Qu'il voulut l'honorer d'une Chevalerie;
    Illustre et noble confrairie
    Moins pleine d'hommes que de Dieux.
L'Amant dit au Demon: c'est ligne circulaire
Et courbe que ceci; je t'ordonne d'en faire
    Ligne droite et sans nuls retours.
    Va t'en-y travailler, et cours.

Promptly to do his will. Thus our compeer
Dispatches him here, there, to do whatever
    Comes to his mind: to raise a storm,
    To build a palace... No endeavor
The all-obeying imp fails to perform.
And in a trice! Soon, through his ministrations,
The beau, with many a ducat in his sack,
Sends him to Rome, whence straightway he comes back
    With pocketfuls of dispensations.
    In short, however far afield he
Sends off the sprite, no chore is too unwieldy.
But soon his brain grows empty of command.
    Confiding his discomfiture
In her, fair object of his *fin amour*,
He tells his tale. "Aha! I understand,"
Cries she. "But, faith, if that is all,
Easily can I snatch that noisome brier
Out of your soul, and wrest you from his thrall:
When next he comes we'll show him who's the slyer!
    Here's something for our demon, sire!
Command him to uncurl it; to unkink it,
    Until it's straight and flat." With this,
She plucked I know not what—although I think it
Came from that mounded grove dubbed "Veneris,"
Whose fleece, that labyrinth of fairy pleasure,
    In ages past, was deemed such treasure
That knighthood claimed its honor for its own.[1]
Says swain to imp (contemptuous is his tone):
    "You see this thing coiled round about?
    I order you to stretch it out,
To make it straight, without the slightest twisting.
    Go! Do it, I command you! Fly!"

L'esprit s'en va; n'a point de cesse

Qu'il n'ait mist le fil sous la presse,

Tâché de l'aplatir à grands coups de marteau,

Fait sejourner au fonds de l'eau;

Sans que la ligne fust d'un seul poinct étenduë;

De quelque tour qu'il se servist,

Quelque secret qu'il eust, quelque charme qu'il fist,

C'estoit temps et peine perduë:

Il ne pût mettre à la raison

La toison.

Elle se revoltoit contre le vent, la pluie,

La neige, le broüillard: plus satan y touchoit

Moins l'annelure se laschoit.

Qu'est-ceci, disoit-il, je ne vis de ma vie

Chose de telle étoffe: il n'est point de lutin

Qui n'y perdist tout son latin.

Messire Diable un beau matin

S'en va trouver son homme, et lui dit: je te laisse.

Aprens-moy seulement ce que c'est que cela:

Je te le rens, tien, le voila,

Je suis victus, je le confesse.

—Nôtre ami Monsieur le luiton,

Dit l'homme, vous perdez un peu trop tost courage;

Celuy-cy n'est pas seul, et plus d'un compagnon

Vous auroit taillé de l'ouvrage.

So fly he does; and try and try
He does as well, struggling, persisting...
  With press... With hammer... Blow by blow...
Soaking it... Pulling, tugging... All to no
  Avail, try though he will; until,
Desisting, he admits that all his skill,
Cunning, and craft are helpless to unfurl
            That curl,
Resisting all the elements together.
Satan himself, as well, would venture whether
He might succeed though sprite had failed thereto:
Alas, the more he ran the ringlet through
His fingers, all the more it coiled and curled.
  Thought he: "Damnable curlicue!
What is it made of? Never in the world...!
No demon would make head or tail, I vow!"
Then, to the beau: "Here. I confess, my ruse
Has come a-cropper. Yes, you win, I lose.
  But this... What is it anyhow?"
And his reply: "Methinks you've lost your touch!
  Give up so soon? Who would have guessed!
And yet, this curl is not the only such:
How might you struggle—many times as much!—
If you had tried to straighten all the rest!"

La Matrone d'Ephèse

S'il est un conte usé, commun, et rebatu,
C'est celuy qu'en ces vers j'accommode à ma guise.
    —Et pourquoy donc le choisis-tu?
    Qui t'engage à cette entreprise?
N'a-t'elle point déja produit assez d'écrits?
    Quelle graçe aura ta Matrone
    Au prix de celle de Pétrone?
Comment la rendras-tu nouvelle à nos esprits?
—Sans répondre aux censeurs, car c'est chose infinie,
Voyons si dans mes Vers je l'auray rajeunie.

    Dans Ephese il fut autrefois
Une Dame en sagesse et vertus sans égale,
    Et selon la commune voix
Ayant sceu rafiner sur l'amour conjugale.
Il n'étoit bruit que d'elle et de sa chasteté:
    On l'alloit voir par rareté:
C'étoit l'honneur du sexe: heureuse sa patrie!
Chaque mere à sa bru l'alleguoit pour Patron;
Chaque époux la prônoit à sa femme cherie;
D'elle desçendent ceux de la prudoterie,
    Antique et celebre maison.
    Son mari l'aimoit d'amour folle.
    Il mourut. De dire comment,
    Ce seroit un détail frivole;
    Il mourut, et son testament
N'étoit plein que de legs qui l'auroient consolée,
Si les biens réparoient la perte d'un mari
    Amoureux autant que cheri.
Mainte veuve pourtant fait la déchevelée,
Qui n'abandonne pas le soin du demeurant,

The Matron of Ephesus

If any tale—well worn, banal—
Needs no retelling, it's the one I shall
 Herewith relate in my own wise.
 "But why?" you ask. "Why re-create her,
That personage of more than one narrator:
The Matron that Petronius glorifies
And many an imitator, too, discusses?[1]
What special grace can you give yours to vie,
 Verily, with Petronius's?"
Rather than face my critics in reply—
 Task of duration infinite!—
 Let me but try to see if I
Can spruce his famous Matron up a bit.

Long years gone by, in Ephesus,
There lived a woman, passing virtuous,
In wifely duty chaste beyond compare:
Pride of her sex, hailed far and wide. And thus
 Came many a soul to see her there,
Eager to gaze upon a sight so rare.
Each mother wished such consort for her son;
Each man wished for a mate like such a one.
(Ancestress of the clan Prudenda, she
 Gave rise to long posterity...[2])
 Her husband loved her madly. But
 He died—no need to say of what
 (Frivolous piece of information!);
 He died: let that suffice—and left
A will that would have brought much consolation
Could wealth console Madame, now sore bereft
Of spouse so loving and so loved. But no,

Et du bien qu'elle aura fait le compte en pleurant.

Celle-cy par ses cris mettoit tout en allarme;
  Celle-cy faisoit un vacarme,
Un bruit, et des regrets à perçer tous les cœurs;
  Bien qu'on sçache qu'en ces malheurs
De quelque desespoir qu'une ame soit atteinte,
La douleur est toûjours moins forte que la plainte,
Toûjours un peu de faste entre parmi les pleurs.
Chacun fit son devoir de dire à l'affligée
Que tout a sa mesure, et que de tels regrets
  Pourroient pécher par leur excés:
Chacun rendit par là sa douleur rengregée.
Enfin ne voulant plus joüir de la clarté
  Que son époux avoit perduë,
Elle entre dans sa tombe, en ferme volonté
D'accompagner cette ombre aux enfers desçenduë.
Et voyez ce que peut l'excessive amitié;
(Ce mouvement aussi va jusqu'à la folie)
Une esclave en ce lieu la suivit par pitié,
  Prête à mourir de compagnie.
Prête, je m'entends bien; c'est à dire en un mot
N'ayant examiné qu'à demi ce complot,
Et jusques à l'effet courageuse et hardie.
L'esclave avec la Dame avoit été nourrie.
Toutes deux s'entraimoient, et cette passion
Etoit cruë avec l'âge au cœur des deux femelles:
Le monde entier à peine eut fourni deux modeles
  D'une telle inclination.

Comme l'esclave avoit plus de sens que la Dame,
Elle laissa passer les premiers mouvemens,
Puis tâcha, mais en vain, de remettre cette ame

Not such a widow, she: such as will crow
    Their grief—hair torn and garments rent—
But who, beating their breast to loud lament,
Add up their riches as they weep their woe.
No, this one moaned and wailed and bellowed so,
That all grew much alarmed and much distressed.
    (Though they assumed that, like the rest,
This widow, while sincere her lamentation,
Was not ungiven to exaggeration,
Just for the show.) And thus they did as best
    They could to temper her chagrin,
Telling Her Widowhood it was a sin
To mourn beyond all proper measure. Yet
    All they accomplished was to whet
The dire despair of our fair heroine,
    And make her grieve, alas, the more;
Until, in time, the poor bereaved forswore
The light of day, loath to participate
In pleasure now denied her lifeless mate.
And so into his tomb went she, intent
    There to remain, and join the late
Lamented in his netherward descent.
With her there went a slave girl, much devoted—
Cradle-companion, close as close could be—
Thither to keep her mistress company
    And die as well; though, be it noted,
    This loving, loyal devotee
("Devoted?" Rather "mad," if you ask me!),
Exemplar of affection sisterly,[3]
Had failed, I fear, to think the matter through.

But soon the servant comes to realize

Dans l'ordinaire train des communs sentimens.
Aux consolations la veuve inaccessible
S'appliquoit seulement à tout moyen possible
De suivre le defunt aux noirs et tristes lieux:
Le fer auroit été le plus court et le mieux,
Mais la Dame vouloit paître encore ses yeux
    Du tresor qu'enfermoit la biere,
    Froide dépoüille, et pourtant chere.
    C'étoit là le seul aliment
    Qu'elle prist en ce monument.
    La faim donc fut celle des portes
    Qu'entre d'autres de tant de sortes,
Nôtre veuve choisit pour sortir d'icy bas.
Un jour se passe, et deux sans autre nourriture
Que ses profonds soûpirs, que ses frequens helas,
    Qu'un inutile et long murmure
Contre les Dieux, le sort, et toute la nature.
    Enfin sa douleur n'obmit rien,
    Si la douleur doit s'exprimer si bien.

Encore un autre mort faisoit sa residence
Non loin de ce tombeau, mais bien differemment,
    Car il n'avoit pour monument
    Que le dessous d'une potence.
Pour exemple aux voleurs on l'avoit là laissé.
    Un Soldat bien recompensé
    Le gardoit avec vigilance.
    Il étoit dit par Ordonnance
Que si d'autres voleurs, un parent, un ami
L'enlevoient, le Soldat nonchalant, endormi
    Rempliroit aussi-tôt sa plaçe,
    Cétoit trop de severité;

What such a stay must needs expose her to.
At first she lets her mistress sigh her sighs
    And groan her groans; then vainly tries
To make her mourn as other widows do,
In manner more conventional withal.
The Matron, though—obdurate, spurning all
The usual consolations—has one thought
    And one alone: what means she ought
    Employ to reach unto that dismal
    Valley of death, domain abysmal.
    Quickest, no doubt, would be the sword.
But she demurs; for she would longer feast
    Her eyes upon the poor deceased—
Cold in his bier, and yet no less adored.
Such being, indeed, the only nourishment
    The mausoleum offers her,
Madame decides that to pursue Monsieur
Starvation is her best expedient:
    Portal direct, through which to quit
This mortal coil and be well rid of it.
    One day... Then two... And she had fed
On nought but her "alas'es" and "ah, me's":
    Long song of woe; duly dispirited,
    Cursing the gods, fate's vagaries,
And all of life's most grave inequities.

    Now, hard by where Monsieur lay dead,
A second corpse hung swinging in the breeze:
    A proper blackguard, and for whom
Only the gibbet—no fine marble tomb—
Would stand to mark his infamous demise;
Left thus, so other thieves might cast their eyes

Mais la publique utilité

Deffendoit que l'on fist au garde aucune grace.

Pendant la nuit il vid aux fentes du tombeau

Briller quelque clarté, spectacle assez nouveau.

Curieux il y court, entend de loin la Dame

Remplissant l'air de ses clameurs.

Il entre, est étonné, demande à cette femme,

Pourquoy ces cris, pourquoy ces pleurs,

Pourquoy cette triste musique,

Pourquoy cette maison noire et melancolique.

Occupée à ses pleurs à peine elle entendit

Toutes ces demandes frivoles,

Le mort pour elle y répondit;

Cet objet sans autres parolles

Disoit assez par quel malheur

La Dame s'enterroit ainsi toute vivante.

Nous avons fait serment, ajoûta la suivante,

De nous laisser mourir de faim et de douleur.

Encor que le soldat fust mauvais orateur,

Il leur fit concevoir ce que c'est que la vie.

La Dame cette fois eut de l'attention;

Et déja l'autre passion

Se trouvoit un peu ralentie.

Le tems avoit agi. Si la foy du serment,

Poursuivit le soldat, vous deffend l'aliment,

Voyez-moy manger seulement,

Vous n'en mourrez pas moins. Un tel temperament

Ne déplut pas aux deux femelles:

Conclusion qu'il obtint d'elles

Une permission d'apporter son soupé;

Ce qu'il fit; et l'esclave eut le cœur fort tenté

Thereon, and be thereby deterred.
A soldier, placed to guard this gallows-bird,
Well paid therefor, did so with anxious care.
     For if, through his neglect—mayhap
     The merest nod or briefest nap—
     Brigands or friends or kin should dare
Come snatch the corpse, then must it be replaced
     By him himself, and that posthaste!
(Punishment most severe, but one that would,
Presumably best serve the common good.)
And so it happens that, indeed, that night
     Said guard espies a beam of light
Slivering through the gloom. Great his surprise
As to the tomb he hies him; stops; hears cries
     Rending the air... Inside he goes:
     Astonished at the sight, he eyes
The grieving widow there, bawling her woes.
     Many his wherefores and his whys:
Why such? Why so?... But so distraught is she
     That she ignores his queries, lets
     The corpse, in mute soliloquy,
Account for her vociferous regrets
And her decision thus to be entombed.
Her slave adds more: "Madame and I are doomed
To starve with grief. For so we swore." Whereat
     The guard, distressed at their condition,
Discourses—though no gilt-tongued rhetorician—
     On life (its meaning, and all that).
The wife gives ear, more willing by the minute;
Hears what he has to say, takes pleasure in it;
Begins to lose her firm resolve... Says he:
     "Starve if you must. I'll not entreat you.

De renoncer délors à la cruelle envie
     De tenir au mort compagnie.
Madame, ce dit-elle, un penser m'est venu:
Qu'importe à vôtre époux que vous cessiez de vivre?
Croyez-vous que luy-méme il fût homme à vous suivre
Si par vôtre trépas vous l'aviez prevenu?
Non Madame, il voudroit achever sa carriere.
La nôtre sera longue encor si nous voulons.
Se faut-il à vingt-ans enfermer dans la biere?
Nous aurons tout loisir d'habiter ces maisons.
On ne meurt que trop tôt; qui nous presse? attendons;
Quant à moy je voudrois ne mourir que ridée.
Voulez-vous emporter vos appas chez les morts?
Que vous servira-t'il d'en être regardée?
     Tantôt en voyant les tresors
Dont le Ciel prit plaisir d'orner vôtre visage,
     Je disois: helas! c'est dommage,
Nous mêmes nous allons enterrer tout cela.
A ce discours flateur la Dame s'éveilla.
Le Dieu qui fait aimer prit son tems; il tira
Deux traits de son carquois; de l'un il entama
Le soldat jusqu'au vif; l'autre effleura la Dame:
Jeune et belle elle avoit sous ses pleurs de l'éclat,
     Et des gens de goût délicat
Auroient bien pû l'aimer, et méme êtant leur femme.
Le garde en fut épris: les pleurs et la pitié,
     Sorte d'amours ayant ses charmes,
Tout y fit: Une belle, alors qu'elle est en larmes
     En est plus belle de moitié.
Voilà donc nôtre veuve écoutant la loüange,
Poison qui de l'amour est le premier degré;

But if you sit and watch me eat, you
   Need die no less, I guarantee.
Pray let me fetch my supper." They agree;
And off he goes, returning with his food.

   As thus he supped and chomped and chewed,
The slave began to harbor much misgiving
   About the cruel vicissitude
Of thus departing from amongst the living
To join Monsieur in death. "Madame," she said,
"The thought occurs to me that, were you dead
And were your husband yet alive, then surely
   There's little question, *entre nous*,
But that he'd not be quick to follow you.
Life is so short: why leave it prematurely?
At twenty years the grave can wait, no worry!
Long will it be our host: so why the hurry?
Me? Let me live till wrinkles fill my face!
What? Would you waste your beauty and your grace
Upon the dead? What pleasure can they give them,
   Imprisoned in their chill embrace?
   Better to let yourself outlive them—
These charms divine of yours—and not allow
The jealous bier too soon to claim them." Now,
The compliments, of course, have their effect:
Madame is quickened, as you might expect,
To thoughts of beauty and, perforce, of love.
   At length, the impish god thereof
Looses an arrow from his quiver at her,
   And at the guard as well. The latter,
Pierced to the heart, is smitten utterly—
   More deeply than, at first, is she.
The more she sobs, the more those teardrops flatter

La voilà qui trouve à son gré
Celuy qui le luy donne; il fait tant qu'elle mange,
Il fait tant que de plaire, et se rend en effet
Plus digne d'être aimé que le mort le mieux fait.
        Il fait tant enfin qu'elle change;
Et toûjours par degrez, comme l'on peut penser:
De l'un à l'autre il fait cette femme passer;
        Je ne le trouve pas étrange:
Elle écoute un amant, elle en fait un mari;
Le tout au nez du mort qu'elle avoit tant cheri.

Pendant cet hymenée un voleur se hazarde
D'enlever le dépost commis aux soins du garde.
Il en entend le bruit; il y court à grands pas;
        Mais en vain, la chose étoit faite.
Il revient au tombeau conter son embarras,
        Ne sçachant où trouver retraite.
L'esclave alors luy dit le voyant éperdu:
        L'on vous a pris vôtre pendu?
Les Loix ne vous feront, dites-vous, nulle grace?
Si Madame y consent j'y remedieray bien.
        Mettons nôtre mort en la place,
        Les passans n'y connoîtront rien.
La Dame y consentit. O volages femelles!
La femme est toûjours femme; il en est qui sont belles,
        Il en est qui ne le sont pas.
        S'il en étoit d'assez fideles,
        Elles auroient assez d'appas.

Prudes vous vous devez défier de vos forces.
Ne vous vantez de rien. Si vôtre intention

The winsome face behind the weeping mask.
(Beauty that even many a husband would
    Find worth the yoke of husbandhood!)
And so the soldier, warming to the task,
    Proceeds to woo the widow, doing
    Everything wooers do a-wooing,
Much to the pleasure of Madame the wooed.
He does so well that, soon, she tastes his food;
So well, that he seems fitter, far, to have her
Than even the most fair and fit cadaver;
So well, that there, before her dear deceased,
Widow turns wife—or so to speak, at least.

But as they lie thus consummating, lo!
A brigand steals that other corpse—the one
Our groom forgets to guard... He'll run... But no,
    Too late, alack! The deed is done...
Back to the tomb, in panic, will he flee
To tell Madame the fell catastrophe.
How can he save his skin? Aye, that's the question!
For which the slave girl, full of sympathy,
    Offers him an untoward suggestion:
"By Madame's leave, no one will know if we
Hang up our corpse to take your corpse's place."
Madame agrees... O woman! Fickle race!
    Some fair; some plain of face and feature;
But faithful? Ah, would there were such a creature!

Prudes, be advised: vaunt not your strength of will
Though your intent be to resist temptation.
    For, fare we well or fare we ill,

Est de resister aux amorçes,
La nôtre est bonne aussi; mais l'execution
Nous trompe également; témoin cette Matrone.
    Et n'en déplaise au bon Petrone,
Ce n'étoit pas un fait tellement merveilleux
Qu'il en dût proposer l'exemple à nos neveux.
Cette veuve n'eut tort qu'au bruit qu'on luy vid faire,
Qu'au dessein de mourir, malconçeu, mal formé;
    Car de mettre au patibulaire,
    Le corps d'un mary tant aimé,
Ce n'étoit pas peut-être une si grande affaire.
Cela luy sauvoit l'autre; et tout consideré,
Mieux vaut goujat debout qu'Empereur enterré.

Strong, too, is man's determination.
Witness our famous Matron, who—
Meaning the good Petronius no offense—
Did, I must say, what many a wife would do
Under the circumstances; and who, hence,
Deserves no exemplary mention.
Her folly? Vowing, in her innocence,
To die entombed: absurd intention!
Nor need she have too long repented
Hanging her dear-departed late-lamented
To save her swain. For, as she would discover,
Better to have a living lover—
Even a varlet, poor and lowly bred—
Than all your kings and emperors, rich but dead.

The Matron of Ephesus

La Clochette

Conte

O combien l'homme est inconstant, divers,
Foible, leger, tenant mal sa parole!
J'avois juré hautement en mes vers
De renoncer à tout conte frivole.
Et quand juré? c'est ce qui me confond,
Depuis deux jours j'ay fait cette promesse:
Puis fiez-vous à Rimeur qui répond
D'un seul moment. Dieu ne fit la sagesse
Pour les cerveaux qui hantent les neuf Sœurs;
Trop bien ont-ils quelque art qui vous peut plaire,
Quelque jargon plein d'assez de douceurs;
Mais d'être sûrs, ce n'est là leur affaire.
Si me faut-il trouver, n'en fût-il point,
Temperament pour accorder ce poinct,
Et supposé que quant à la matiere
J'eusse failly, du moins pourrois-je pas
Le reparer par la forme en tout cas?
Voyons cecy. Vous sçaurez que naguere
Dans la Touraine un jeune Bachelier,
(Interpretez ce mot à vôtre guise,
L'usage en fut autrefois familier
Pour dire ceux qui n'ont la barbe grise,
Ores ce sont supposts de sainte Eglise)
Le nôtre soit sans plus un jouvenceau,
Qui dans les prez, sur le bord d'un ruisseau,
Vous cajoloit la jeune bachelette
Aux blanches dents, aux pieds nuds, au corps gent.
Pendant qu'Io portant une clochette,
Aux environs alloit l'herbe mangeant,

The Cowbell

How changeable is man! How vain his vow!
Weak, fickle, undependable, and worse...
Myself, I plainly swore that, in my verse,
I would forswear the trivial tale. But now
I wonder when. (What's more, I wonder how.)
Two days ago, perhaps? Well, if I swore...[1]
But careful lest you trust a rhymester's oath,
Pledged on the moment. God, I fear, was loath
To vest good sense and wisdom, heretofore,
In brains beset—bemused?—by Sisters Nine.
So much would poets tell, in tongue so fine;
But keep their word? Unlikely, not much more.
Now, such a one as I, shall I keep mine?
Try though I might, yet would I find some way
To compromise; so that, should what I say
Fall short, at least the manner of the telling
Could nonetheless redeem the matter told.
In proof whereof, I ask that you behold
A *bachelier* who, in Touraine, was dwelling
Off in the country. (*Bachelier*: a word
In the familiar language, often heard,
Times past, to signify a beardless youth.
No more; though now we use the term, in truth,
To mean one of your lackey Church-hound sorts...)
Forsooth, this *bachelier* of ours is merely
A swain of callow years, who, cavalierly
Dallying by the brooklet's edge, disports
In frolicsome flirtation: many's the lass—
White-toothed, fair, bare of foot—whom he exhorts
To play at love... Now then, it comes to pass

Nôtre galand vous lorgne une fillette,
De celles-là que je viens d'exprimer:
Le malheur fut qu'elle étoit trop jeunette,
Et d'âge encore incapable d'aimer.
Non qu'à treize ans on y soit inhabile;
Même les loix ont avancé ce temps:
Les loix songeoient aux personnes de ville,
Bien que l'amour semble né pour les champs.
Le Bachelier déploya sa science:
Ce fut en vain; le peu d'experience,
L'humeur farouche, ou bien l'aversion,
Ou tous les trois, firent que la bergere,
Pour qui l'amour étoit langue étrangere,
Répondit mal à tant de passion.
Que fit l'amant? croyant tout artifice
Libre en amours, sur le rez de la nuit
Le compagnon détourne une genisse
De ce bétail par la fille conduit;
Le demeurant, non conté par la belle,
(Jeunesse n'a les soins qui sont requis)
Prit aussi-tôt le chemin du logis;
Sa mere étant moins oublieuse qu'elle,
Vid qu'il manquoit une piece au Troupeau:
Dieu sçait la vie; elle tance Isabeau,
Vous la renvoye, et la jeune pucelle
S'en va pleurant, et demande aux échos
Si pas un d'eux ne sçait nulle nouvelle
De celle-là dont le drôle à propos
Avoit d'abord étoupé la clochette;
Puis il la prit, et la faisant sonner
Il se fit suivre, et tant que la fillette

That, as he dawdles, lolling on the grass,
One of those tender maidens that I mention—
Tending her herd, bell-necked as cows will be—[2]
Attracts our lover's amorous attention.
But woe betides the lad—alas!—for she
Is far too tender still for love. Not that,
At thirteen years, maids lack the skill thereat;
Even the laws permit that age today.[3]
(Such laws were made for city folk; in fact,
Love is a country thing!) Our *bachelier*,
At any rate, tried all his wiles, his tact,
His wit... In vain. She would have none of it.
And why, you wonder, would she not submit?
Ah, who can say? A lack of savoir-faire?
Repugnance? Petulance? Perhaps all three.
Well, be that as it may, the young *bergère*,
Unmoved, leaves him alone to languish there:
Unused to lover's language, she! And he?
Convinced that any ruse is fair in love,
He waits for night to fall, then leads astray
A heifer from the herd, mentioned above.
The rest, uncounted—for our young obey
No rules of common sense!—lumber away.
The mother, though, counting the sum thereof
When they return, discovers one too few;
Gives Isabeau a proper talking-to;
And sends her back to try to find the heifer.
Weeping, she wanders all the twilight through,
Asking the echoes and the gentle zephyr
If any may have seen the beast—whose bell
The beau had deadened, unbeknownst to her!

Au fonds d'un bois se laissa détourner.
Jugez, Lecteur, quelle fut sa surprise
Quand elle oüit la voix de son amant.
Belle, dit-il, toute chose est permise
Pour se tirer de l'amoureux tourment;
A ce discours, la fille toute en transe
Remplit de cris ces lieux peu frequentez;
Nul n'accourut. O belles évitez
Le fonds des bois et leur vaste silence.

At length he rings it, and our sly young sir
Is followed by our artless damosel
Into the wood. Imagine her surprise
When there he stands, saying, despite her cries:
"My love, all's fair to ease my heart's chagrin."
She calls for help, but no soul dwells therein.
And no one comes. The night its secret keeps...
Maids, shun the wood and flee its silent deeps.

Le Fleuve Scamandre

Conte

Me voila prest à conter de plus belle;
Amour le veut, et rit de mon serment:
Hommes et Dieux, tout est sous sa tutelle;
Tout obeit, tout cede à cet enfant:
J'ay desormais besoin en le chantant
De traits moins forts, et déguisans la chose:
Car aprés tout, je ne veux être cause
D'aucun abus: que plûtôt mes écrits
Manquent de sel, et ne soient d'aucun prix!
Si dans ces vers j'introduis et je chante
Certain trompeur et certaine innocente,
C'est dans la veuë et dans l'intention
Qu'on se meffie en telle occasion:
J'ouvre l'esprit, et rends le sexe habile
A se garder de ces pieges divers.
Sotte ignorance en fait trebucher mille,
Contre une seule à qui nuiroient mes vers.

J'ay lû qu'un Orateur estimé dans la Grece,
Des beaux Arts autrefois souveraine Maîtresse,
Banni de son pays, voulut voir le séjour
Où subsistoient encor les ruïnes de Troye;
Cimon, son camarade, eut sa part de la joye.
Du débris d'Ilion s'étoit construit un bourg
Noble par ces malheurs; là Priam et sa Cour
N'étoient plus que des noms, dont le Temps fait sa proye.
Ilion, ton nom seul a des charmes pour moy;
Lieu fécond en sujets propres à nôtre employ.
Ne verray-je jamais rien de toy, ny la place
De ces murs élevez et détruits par des Dieux,

The River Scamander

Now shall I tell my tales again;
For Love insists, and mocks my oath.[1]
Cupid: that lord of gods and men—
Mere child, but master of them both.
But loath am I to scandalize;
And so, hereafter, shall I try
To show him in less wicked wise,
Even if in my verse, thereby,
I must be satisfied to write
With much less spice and not much bite.
Now, here, if yet again I sing
Of lying rogue and sweet young thing,
It's to prevent our ladyfriends
From falling, trapped, and faltering:
Such my intent and motive humble.
For each fair maid my verse offends,
Ignorance makes a thousand stumble.

An orator in Greece[2]—rich fountainhead
Of ancient arts—having, in time, been banished,
Set out, intending (so, at least, I've read)
To view the ruins of a Troy long vanished.
Cimon, a friend, accompanied his quest.
On Ilium's remains there stood a town,
Still woe-enshrined. There, Priam and the rest
Were nought but names: Time's prey. But your renown,
O Troy!, still crowns the space; and, yet again
Today, inspires and prods the poet's pen.
What? Shall I never see your walls, cast down
By gods who raised them up?[3] No merest trace,

Ny ces champs où couroient la fureur et l'audace,
Ny des temps fabuleux enfin la moindre trace,
Qui pût me presenter l'image de ces lieux?
Pour revenir au fait, et ne point trop m'étendre,
  Cimon le Heros de ces vers
   Se promenoit prés du Scamandre.
Une jeune ingenuë en ce lieu se vient rendre,
Et goûter la fraîcheur sur ces bords toûjours verts.
Son voile au gré des vens va flotant dans les airs;
Sa parure est sans art; elle a l'air de bergere,
Une beauté naïve, une taille legere.
Cimon en est surpris, et croit que sur ces bords
Venus vient étaler ses plus rares trésors.
Un antre étoit auprés: l'innocente pucelle
Sans soupçon y descend, aussi simple que belle.
Le chaud, la solitude, et quelque Dieu malin
L'inviterent d'abord à prendre un demi bain.
Nôtre banni se cache: il contemple, il admire,
  Il ne sçait quels charmes élire;
Il devore des yeux et du cœur cent beautez.
Comme on étoit remply de ces Divinitez
  Que la Fable a dans son Empire,
Il songe à profiter de l'erreur de ces temps,
Prend l'air d'un Dieu des eaux, moüille ses vétemens,
Se couronne de joncs, et d'herbe degoutante,
Puis invoque Mercure, et le Dieu des Amans:
Contre tant de trompeurs qu'eût fait une innocente?
La belle enfin découvre un pied dont la blancheur
  Auroit fait honte à Galatée,
  Puis le plonge en l'onde argentée,

Fair Troy, of your defiance, your disgrace,
Your fabled battlefields? Your wiles, your woes,
Your fury? What? Destroyed forever, those
Noble reminders of a hallowed place?
But I digress... The hero of my story—
Cimon—was, by the banks of the Scamander,[4]
  Ambling in manner dilatory,
  When lo! a-bloom with youthful candor
And artless naïveté, a lass draws near,
Taking the air amid its cool, green shade,
Veils billowing in the breeze. Seeing her, here—
Lissome of form, unfiligreed—appear
Like humble shepherdess, he thinks the maid
Is goddess Venus, come, indeed, to show
The rarest of her treasures here below.
There was a hollow in the rocks. The child,
Our virgin yet untouched, perhaps beguiled
By roguish god—more likely by the heat,
Thinking herself alone—thought it was meet
To bathe a bit therein. The lad—concealed—
  Peered, ogled, and admired, athirst
  For all the beauties thus revealed,
And barely knew which one to gaze on first,
  Drinking them in with eye and heart.
The time was still when Fable's simple art
Peopled the world with scores of deities:
  Demigods, nymphs, and sprites, and such.
Now, Cimon knew it need not cost him much
To profit from beliefs the likes of these.
And so, wetting his clothes, he weaves his tresses
With dripping reed and weed, prays Mercury,
And Cupid too! Against a panoply

Et regarde ses lys, non sans quelque pudeur.
Pendant qu'à cet objet sa veüe est arrétée,
Cimon aproche d'elle: elle court se cacher
  Dans le plus profond du rocher.
Je suis, dit-il, le Dieu qui commande à cette onde;
Soyez-en la Déesse, et regnez avec moy.
Peu de Fleuves pourroient dans leur grotte profonde
Partager avec vous un aussi digne employ:
Mon cristal est tres-pur, mon cœur l'est davantage:
Je couvriray pour vous de fleurs tout ce rivage,
Trop heureux si vos pas le daignent honorer,
Et qu'au fonds de mes eaux vous daigniez vous mirer.
  Je rendray toutes vos Compagnes
  Nymphes aussi, soit aux montagnes,
Soit aux eaux, soit aux bois, car j'étends mon pouvoir
Sur tout ce que vôtre œil à la ronde peut voir.
L'éloquence du Dieu, la peur de luy déplaire,
Malgré quelque pudeur qui gâtoit le mystere,
  Conclurent tout en peu de temps.
La superstition cause mille accidents.
On dit même qu'Amour intervint à l'affaire.
Tout fier de ce succés le Banni dit adieu.
  Revenez, dit-il, en ce lieu:
  Vous garderez que l'on ne sçache
  Un hymen qu'il faut que je cache:
Nous le declarerons quand j'en auray parlé
Au conseil qui sera dans l'Olimpe assemblé.
La nouvelle Déesse à ces mots se retire;
Contente? Amour le sçait. Un mois se passe et deux,
Sans que pas un du bourg s'apperceût de leurs jeux.
O mortels! est-il dit qu'à force d'être heureux

Of such deceits, what chance have shepherdesses!
At length she bares an ivory foot—so white
That Galatea would have blushed with spite—⁵
   Dips it into the silvery wave,
And sits, in rather decorous inspection
   Of chaste and lilylike perfection.
Just then, Cimon steps forth. She spies the knave,
Runs, finds the deepmost corner of the cave,
   And tries to hide. In vain: he follows.
"Fear not! I am the river-god!" he holloes.
"Come thou, my river-goddess. Reign supreme.
For no divinity of any stream,
River, or brook, who shall thy better be!
Crystal, my water; pure, my heart as well.
   With daffodil and asphodel
Shall I bestrew my banks to honor thee,
Wouldst thou but deign to tread and gaze on me!
   Thy friends shall nymphets be no less:
Of waters, mountains, woods... For I possess
Dominion over all this vast domain:
My realm, my wilderness! Come, love. Come, reign!"
A twinge of chastity... But acquiesce
She does; thanks to her godlet's eloquence—
   And fear, perchance, to give offense.
   For such the strength of superstition
(And, some say, even Cupid's influence).
   Proud now of his successful mission,
Cimon—not yet disposed to travel on—
Invites his goddess to come back anon.
"But careful lest you breathe a word—beware!—
That we are wed! For first must I declare
The deed to all Olympus. Thereupon,

Vous ne le soyez plus! le Banni, sans rien dire,
Ne va plus visiter cet antre si souvent.
  Une nopce enfin arrivant,
Tous pour la voir passer sous l'orme se vont rendre.
La Belle apperçoit l'homme, et crie en ce moment:
  Ah! voila le fleuve Scamandre.
On s'étonne, on la presse, elle dit bonnement
Que son hymen se va conclure au Firmament;
On en rit; car que faire? aucuns à coups de pierre
Poursuivirent le Dieu qui s'enfuit à grand'erre:
D'autres rirent sans plus. Je croy qu'en ce temps-cy
L'on feroit au Scamandre un tres-méchant party.
  En ce temps-là semblables crimes
S'excusoient aisément: tous temps, toutes maximes.
L'épouse du Scamandre en fut quitte à la fin,
  Pour quelques traits de raillerie;
Même un de ses amans l'en trouva plus jolie:
C'est un goust: Il s'offrit à luy donner la main:
Les Dieux ne gâtent rien: puis quand ils seroient cause
Qu'une fille en valût un peu moins, dotez-la,
  Vous trouverez qui la prendra:
  L'argent repare toute chose.

Tell it we may." Whereon the maiden, new
　　To godhead as to love, withdrew.
Happy? Ask Cupid!... Well, a month or two
Went by, and no one in the whole town knew
Their play... But, fickle Man! For soon, forswearing
　　His facile joy, the gallant takes
A bride; and, as the wedding party makes
　　Its way along, our goddess, staring,
Spies him and cries: "The river-god! Scamander!
My husband! That is... Mount Olympus... Later..."
Everyone laughs. But once they understand her,
　　Some stone her vile prevaricator;
But most guffaw. Today, those who philander
Would have the law to answer to...[6] But, ah!
Back then, mere bagatelle! *O tempora*...
As for the belle of our Scamandering bounder,
Jeering and jibe are all she need withstand.
Indeed, one of her lovers even found her
Lovelier for her feat, and sought her hand.
Question of taste... The gods are harmless. Still,
　　Should one do damsel modest ill,
Dower the maid: she'll prove some swain's delight.
Rare is the wrong that money fails to right.

Conte tiré d'Athenée

Du temps des grecs, deux sœurs disoient avoir
Aussi beau cul que filles de leur sorte;
La question ne fut que de savoir
Quelle des deux dessus l'autre l'emporte:
Pour en juger un expert estant pris,
A la moins jeune il accorde le prix,
Puis l'espousant, luy fait don de son ame;
A son exemple, un sien frere est épris
De la cadette, et la prend pour sa femme;
Tant fut entreux, à la fin, procédé,
Que par les sœurs un temple fut fondé,
Dessous le nom de vénus belle-fesse;
Je ne sais pas à quelle intention;
Mais c'eust esté le temple de la gréce
Pour qui j'eusse eû plus de devotion.

Tale from Athenaeus

In ancient Greece two sisters claimed to be,
Of any women born, the fairest-assed.
But of the two, the problem was to see
Which of the lovely-buttocked pair surpassed
The other. Thus an expert in such matter
Was called to weigh the merits of them both:
Younger or elder. He adjudged the latter;
Then made the maid his wife, plighting his troth.
A brother, in his footsteps, who became
Enamored of the former, did the same.
In gratitude the two wives consecrated
A sacred temple duly dedicated
To Venus of the Comely Rump. What for?
Who knows? But of all Grecian shrines created,
In that one would I worship evermore.

Tale from Athenaeus

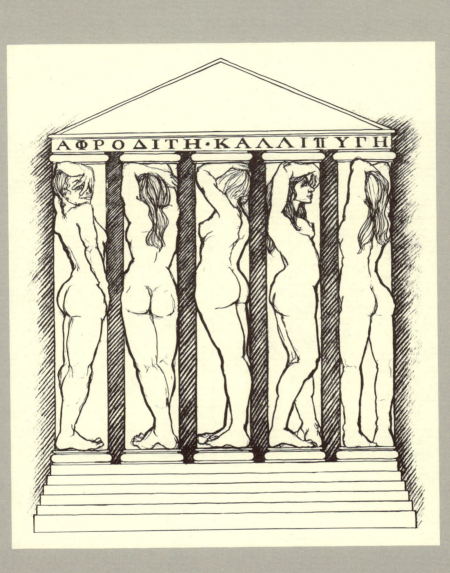

Notes

Prologue

1. The publication of La Fontaine's *Fables* spanned almost three decades: Books 1–6, 1668; Books 7–11, 1678–79; and Book 12, 1694. His *Contes et nouvelles en vers* were published in a variety of groupings, beginning in 1664 and extending through 1685, with several appearing posthumously. (See, inter alia, the chronology in the Ferrier and Collinet edition [Paris: Garnier-Flammarion, 1980], pp. 7–13, for dates of specific collections.) Regarding the many French verse fabulists who have followed in his wake, see my collection, *The Fabulists French: Verse Fables of Nine Centuries* (Urbana: University of Illinois Press, 1992).

2. After a certain amount of politicking and infighting La Fontaine was elected to the Académie in 1683; and then, it is said, only after assuring the Powers That Were that he would be a good boy. According to some sources, his election followed a letter in which he promised to renounce the genre, considered overly and overtly licentious by a number of prelate-academicians and others. Charles Perrault, of "Mother Goose Tales" fame, recounts: "Il estoit de l'Academie Françoise, & lorsqu'il témoigna souhaitter d'en estre, il écrivit une Lettre à un Prelat de la Compagnie, où il marquoit & le déplaisir de s'estre laissé aller à une telle licence, & la resolution où il estoit de ne plus composer rien de semblable" [He was a member of the Académie Française; and when he signified his desire to become one, he wrote a letter to a prelate in that body, in which he expressed both his regret at having indulged himself in such licentiousness and his resolve never again to compose anything of the sort]. (See *Les Hommes illustres qui ont paru en France pendant ce siècle*, 2 vols. [Paris: Antoine Dezallier, 1696–1700], vol. 1, p. 84.)

3. Two contemporaries among the many will suffice as examples. Perrault, for one, precedes the passage cited in n. 2 with the judgment that, in the *Contes*, "Les Images de l'Amour y sont si vives qu'il y a peu de Lectures plus dangereuses pour la Jeunesse, quoyque personne n'ayt jamais parlé plus honnestement des choses deshonnestes" [The portrayals of love are so vivid that few works are more dangerous for youth to read, although no one has ever discussed indecorous subjects in a more decorous manner]. And for another, the acerbic poet and commentator on the arts François Gacon ("Le Poète Sans Fard") complained that, while the *Fables* gained the admiration of decent folk and libertines alike, the *Contes* won the praises of the latter only, "& bien plus parce qu'ils flattent leurs passions, qu'à cause de leur élégance Poetique" [and much more because they tickle their passions than for their poetic elegance].

(See *Homère vengé, ou Réponse à M. De La Motte sur l'Iliade* [Paris: Étienne Ganeau, 1715], p. 112.) Even more recently, poet Paul Valéry, from whom one might expect better, railed at La Fontaine's "vers d'une facilité répugnante" [repugnantly facile verse] in the *Contes*, though probably more for its style than its content. (See John Clarke Lapp, *The Esthetics of Negligence* [Cambridge: Cambridge University Press, 1971], p. 159.)

4. We are told secondhand, by La Fontaine's confessor père Poujet, as recounted by the abbé d'Olivet, that the poet claimed on this occasion that, abjuration notwithstanding, he had really never considered his *Contes* to be "un ouvrage si pernicieux" [such a pernicious work]. (See Ferrier and Collinet, p. 13.)

5. The term *vers libres* ("free verse") should be understood in its seventeenth-century context, not as used in more modern times. The form—perfected by La Fontaine, though occasionally used by contemporaries like Corneille and Molière—while forsaking the rigid regularity of set line-lengths, remains bound by certain conventional constraints of meter and rhyme. Regarding the one-act comedy, *Clymène* (which not all collections of the *Contes et nouvelles en vers* contain), La Fontaine, in a brief prefatory note, defends its unexpected inclusion in his narrative work on the grounds, first, that it concludes with the telling of a lengthy *conte* by the protagonist; and, second, that it was not written to be performed anyway.

6. From the *Avertissement* to his first collection, dating from 1664.

7. Catherine Grisé, in her article devoted to La Fontaine's successors in the genre ("Le Jeu de l'imitation..."), indicates along with other pertinent details that, over the generations, a number of apocryphal tales were, in fact, even attributed to him.

8. La Fontaine's observation follows directly on the passage quoted above, referred to in n. 6.

Le Cocu, battu, et content

1. The noun *cadet*, in the original, literally means "youngest." But since the youngest son of most less-than-wealthy families of the period was traditionally destined for the Church, it came to be used, as here, with ecclesiastical connotation.

Conte d'une chose arrivée à Chasteau-Thierry

1. I do not attempt, in my translation, to get involved in the intricacies of archaic weights and measures. Perfectionists concerned with exactitude may take comfort in the knowledge that a *mi-muid* (here: *my-muid*) of grain—half a hogshead—was the equivalent, roughly, of two and a half liters at the time. (See the Ferrier and Collinet edition of the *Contes* [Paris: Garnier-Flammarion, 1980], p. 417.)

Conte tiré d'Athenée

1. The reader will note the liberty I have taken with La Fontaine's characteristically suggestive image, centering on the verb *pondre* ("to lay eggs"), substituting one that, no less suggestive, is perhaps more appropriate, given the sex of the two seducers.

Le Faiseur d'oreilles et le racommodeur de moules

1. The suggestion, at least implicit—and perhaps clearer in the translation than in the original—is that Sire Guillaume would have a pair of dreaded horns that he hadn't counted on.

La Servante justifiée

1. Many would dispute the appropriateness of La Fontaine's epithet *divin* applied to the ribald Boccaccio. Clearly he is referring to the artistic skill of the famous *conteur* and not to the subjects of his inspiration.

2. The allusion is obviously to the anonymous prose collection *Cent Nouvelles Nouvelles* (ca. 1462), modeled mainly on Boccaccio, from which La Fontaine and others borrowed generously, and quite different in its licentious style and spirit from Marguerite de Navarre's posthumous *Heptaméron* (1558)—source of the present tale (Cinquième Journée, no. 45), as he proceeds to indicate—more prolix and philosophical in its treatment of the no-less-suggestive narratives.

3. La Fontaine's reference to Marguerite's "*c'estoit moi*" will become clear in the concluding dialogue, a faithful adaptation of the corresponding scene in her tale, in which the phrase is repeated several times in comedic fashion reminiscent of Molière.

4. The expression *(de) bonne rob(b)e*, in the original, is a sixteenth-century term with a variety of meanings, ranging from "corpulent" to "of high quality," analogous to the Italian *buona* (or *bella*) *roba* ("fine piece," "nice article").

5. My unorthodox use of a single rhyme in three successive lines—certainly not typical of La Fontaine's prosody, for all its liberties, though occasionally met with—reflects the original, where I think it can be assumed to be no less intentional than in my version.

Le Calendrier des vieillards

1. La Fontaine, understandably, Gallicizes the name of the Italian original, Ricciardo di Chinzica, as well as—rather more capriciously—those of the two other principals, Paganino da Monaco (or da Mare) and Bartolomea Gualandi, below. While the Italian family names are, indeed, known to historians, his assertion of the specific judge's fame, un-

suggested in Boccaccio (*Decameron* 2.10), would seem a gratuitous paren-
thesis, pretext for a typical collusive aside to the reader.

2. Even before La Fontaine's time, when its name was entering the
language as a synonym for great wealth, Peru had come to be taken as
prototypical of any exotic, almost otherworldly civilization.

3. I have not resisted putting into the pompous old man's mouth this
deliciously absurd observation, not literally present in La Fontaine's
original, but not out of keeping, I think, with its spirit.

L'Anneau d'Hans Carvel

1. The curiously abbreviated provenance refers to Rabelais, the third
book of whose Gargantuan and Pantgruelian chronicles contains the
present suggestive anecdote (chap. 27). (Several of La Fontaine's editors
give considerable additional information regarding its appearance in
other narratives as well.)

Le Gascon puny

1. The Gascons have a reputation among the French for their brag-
gadocio and bluster, as have the Normans, to whom La Fontaine will
allude below, for their shrewdness. See, for example, the opening lines
of his celebrated version of the Aesopic fable "The Fox and the Grapes":
"Certain Renard gascon, d'autres disent normand, / Mourant presque de
faim, vit au haut d'une treille / Des Raisins mûrs . . ." (3.11).

L'Hermite

1. While La Fontaine refers simply to hermits, it is plain from what
follows that he is not aiming his ridicule at mere secular recluses. An
earlier version of the *conte*, from 1667, makes the religious implication
perfectly clear from the outset, specifying monks instead of hermits.
(See the Ferrier and Collinet edition of the *Contes* [Paris: Garnier-Flam-
marion, 1980], p. 429.) My translation is a compromise between both
versions.

2. Maistre Gonin was a celebrated magician of the sixteenth century,
whose adeptness at trickery and stratagem, becoming legendary, had
virtually turned his name (often even written without capitals) into a
common noun by La Fontaine's day.

3. On La Fontaine's (and my) use of a single rhyme in three successive
lines, see "La Servante justifiée," n. 5).

4. Clearly La Fontaine's Miserere is not the same as a Hail Mary. But
the point at issue in the original is the brevity of the prayer, not its
content. The Latin word *miserere* was, indeed, coming to be used in the
French of this period to mean a short space of time.

5. According to a long-held (and, in some popular quarters, still-held) old wives' superstition, eating two eggs would guarantee the birth of a male child, for anatomically symbolic reasons not hard to deduce.

Le Bast

1. The suggestive resonances of the final lines of the translation, if not wholly faithful to the letter of the original, are certainly consonant with its spirit.

Comment l'esprit vient aux filles

1. Lest anyone suspect me of a gross and unwonted anachronism, I hasten to mention that the use of the adjective "foul," as applied to various games and sports, antedates its use in baseball vocabulary by several centuries.

2. The noun *marchand(e)* could designate both a seller and, as here, a buyer, though the latter meaning had already grown rather archaic. It is no doubt for that reason that La Fontaine intentionally used it, imparting here, as throughout his text, an antique flavor to the *Contes*.

3. In La Fontaine's defense it should be pointed out that no equivalent of the dubious interlinguistic pun on the verb "inculcate" exists in his original.

4. The "Phœbé" in question, in the original, does not appear to have anything to do with classical mythology, but is probably derived from the name for the *gâteau des Rois*, the Christmas cake, containing its prize bean, or *fève*. At least that is the origin suggested by Ferrier and Collinet on p. 441 of their edition of the *Contes* (Paris: Garner-Flammarion, 1980), supplementing—and differing slightly from—information offered by Henri Regnier, Pierre Clarac, and other editors.

Le Psautier

1. As La Fontaine admits, with none-too-convincing semicontrition, he cannot resist following many a Gallic and other predecessor in poking fun at the *bonnes sœurs*. The three tales referred to in his enumeration are "Mazet de Lamporechio" and a pair included in the present collection: "Conte de ****" (pp. 30–31) and "L'Abbesse" (pp. 150–59). After professing to treat the subject here "pour la dernière fois," he will exploit it yet twice more: in "Les Lunettes" (pp. 200–213) and "Le Tableau."

2. Unlike Boccaccio's hero (*Decameron* 9.2), La Fontaine's young man seems to have rather easy access to the convent; an unusual circumstance that the poet makes no attempt to explain.

3. I permit myself here a translator's license: the minor but irresistible exegetical parenthesis on the specific purpose of the laces in question.

La Jument du compère Pierre

1. La Fontaine appears to be punning here on the expression *prêcher sur la vendange* ("to preach on the grape harvest"), though there is disagreement as to its meaning. Contemporary lexicographer Richelet, in his *Dictionnaire françois* (1680), tells us that it means "to speak only of wine, of drinking," and cites this passage as an example. The venerable Littré, on the other hand, in his latter-day *Dictionnaire de la langue française* (1863–73), also citing the passage, gives quite a different meaning: "to hold one's glass in hand and pass the time talking instead of drinking." As for the lines that follow, they are also rather obscure (La Fontaine's protestation of clarity notwithstanding), though I think it can be assumed that the other subject of the *curé*'s sermons, of special interest to the young, must be sex. At any rate, my translation attempts to respect the several ambiguities.

2. The French have long found the Gaelic languages of Brittany most impenetrable. Enough so to be used, as here, to typify the unintelligible; although the more common equivalent of our "It's all Greek" invokes not Breton—high or low—but Hebrew ("C'est de l'hébreu").

3. Readers of the *Decameron* (9.10) will appreciate how much more explicit Boccaccio is in this passage than a rather timid La Fontaine, whose version is even somewhat less graphic than my own.

Pasté d'anguille

1. As in "La Servante justifiée" and "L'Hermite" (see nn. 5 and 3), my three successive identical rhymes echo La Fontaine's similar unorthodox usage of a few lines above ("friand / autant / apprends").

2. I leave it to the reader to explicate La Fontaine's tongue-in-cheek reference to the lady's little dog: what he needs to be persuaded of, and, indeed, how money can do the persuading.

Les Lunettes

1. See "Le Psautier," pp. 162–63.

2. The original, invoking the bucolically prototypical "Robin," is proverbial, apparently first coined by the *conteur* Bonaventure Des Périers in his posthumous *Nouvelles Récréations et joyeux devis* (1558), source of much of La Fontaine's narrative inspiration.

3. Several editors—Henri Regnier, most detailed among them (*Œuvres complètes de Jean de la Fontaine*, 11 vols. [Paris: Hachette, 1883–92], vol. 5, p. 519)—give as the antecedents for La Fontaine's lengthy allegory (supposedly of Oriental origin, and touched on obliquely in Plato's *Symposium* [189–93]) François Béroalde de Verville's

salacious *Le Moyen de parvenir* (1610), chap. 43, as well as satiric works by his contemporaries, the actor Deslauriers (alias Bruscambille) and the celebrated huckster Tabarin.

4. I think it safe to assume, given the context, that La Fontaine, in his description of this "procession," intended a wordplay on *verges* ("sticks") and *vierges* ("virgins"). If he didn't, he should have. (Hence the pun in my translation.) Myself, I would avoid reading a phallic interpretation into the passage, despite the anatomical subject matter and the long-standing slang meaning of *verge*. But more ingenious interpreters may well find it reasonable to do so.

5. Nicole Ferrier and Jean-Pierre Collinet (in their edition of the *Contes et nouvelles en vers* [Paris: Garnier-Flammarion, 1980], p. 450) suggest that the three dots in La Fontaine's text, between the pronoun *je* and the verb *feray*, were intended to invite the reader to substitute a more vulgar word; no doubt the taboo *foutrai*, which they do not feel the need to specify.

Le Cuvier

1. The Louvre, from its modest beginnings as a medieval hunting-lodge, had, through successive addition, been metamorphosed into a royal palace. It remained so in La Fontaine's time, not becoming a museum, at least in large part, until the last years of the eighteenth-century.

2. See "Comment l'esprit vient aux filles," n. 2.

3. Perhaps through confusion with the term *bonne foi* ("good faith"), the expression *avoir bon foie* ("to have a good liver") was applied to gullible husbands. (See Nicole Ferrier's and Jean-Pierre Collinet's edition of the *Contes* [Paris: Garnier-Flammarion, 1980], p. 451.) Pierre Clarac, in his edition of the *Contes* (2 vols. [Paris: Sociéte les Belles Lettres, 1934], vol. 2, p. 310), explains it as a simple reference to an absence of the bilious humor, as reflected in the idiom *se faire de la bile* ("to fret"). My translation, at any rate, attempts to preserve a generally anatomical, not to say culinary, implication.

La Chose impossible

1. I have preserved La Fontaine's tongue-in-cheek protestation of innocence, but have, in the ensuing passage, paraphrased somewhat the mythological and historical allusions. Cypris is, of course, one of the several names for Venus, deriving from the cult of Aphrodite on Cyprus. As for the "duc" in question, the reference is to King Philippe le Bon, who, as Duc de Bourgogne, in 1429, founded the Ordre de la Toison d'Or ("Order of the Golden Fleece").

La Matrone d'Ephèse

1. The story, taken from Petronius's *Satyricon* (111–12), was, in fact, subsequently treated by numerous authors, French and otherwise, several of whom are cited in Nicole Ferrier's and Jean-Pierre Collinet's edition of the *Contes* ([Paris: Garnier-Flammarion, 1980], pp. 452–53). La Fontaine himself would seem to have been inspired by it years before, at least obliquely, in his fable "La Jeune Veuve" (6.21).

2. La Fontaine's reference, mildly deformed in my version, is to the family from which the pretentious Madame de Sotenville proudly claims descent in Molière's comedy *Georges Dandin*.

3. Again, as in several previous instances (see "La Servante justifiée," n. 5; "L'Hermite," n. 3; and "Pasté d'anguille," n. 1), my use of a single rhyme over three consecutive lines is justified by La Fontaine's own example, here a dozen lines below ("lieux / mieux / yeux").

La Clochette

1. According to some sources, La Fontaine's controversial election to the Académie Française in 1683 was, indeed, accompanied by a letter in which he promised to renounce the present genre, considered licentious by a number of prelate-academicians and others. (See Prologue, n. 2.)

2. In the original, Io, princess of Argos, was one of Zeus's many mistresses. Turned into a heifer, she was tormented by jealous wife Hera's gadfly, eventually fleeing to Egypt and reassuming human form.

3. An ordinance had, in fact, been passed in 1693 establishing the marriageable age for females as twelve.

Le Fleuve Scamandre

1. See "La Clochette," n. 1.

2. The orator in question would seem to be Aeschines, contemporary of Demosthenes. (See the Ferrier and Collinet edition of the *Contes* [Paris: Garnier-Flammarion, 1980], p. 454.)

3. The reader will recall that Troy, which owed its birth to Apollo and Poseidon, owed its ultimate demise to the antagonism of Hera and Athena—unsuccessful claimants to Discord's golden apple—whose loathing of Paris, abductor of Helen (she of the thousand-ship-launching face), led to the Trojan War.

4. The Scamander is the name of the Trojan river, also dubbed the Xanthos ("golden red") by Homer, for reasons variously hypothesized by Pliny and others. Virgins about to marry were said to bathe in it the day before to honor the river-god with their virginity.

5. The allusion to Galatea—Greek suggesting "milk-white"—refers to the beautiful water-nymph in Homer, in love with Acis and pursued by

the Cyclops Polyphemus, later immortalized in Ovid's *Metamorphoses* and in Handel's masque *Acis and Galatea* (1718). (It is of incidental interest to note, that she had also inspired La Fontaine's unfinished—and undistinguished—pastoral *Galatée*, published along with his *Poème de Quinquina* in 1682, three years before the publication of the present *conte*.) Temptation to see, no less logically, another ivory-hued Galatea as the referent is countered by the fact that the statue-turned-woman, heroine of the Pygmalion legend, apparently did not receive her name until many decades after La Fontaine, baptised, it would appear, by Rousseau in his "scène lyrique" *Pygmalion*, first performed in 1770.

6. As Ferrier and Collinet point out (p. 454), in La Fontaine's time his divine impersonator could have been prosecuted for both *libertinage* and *sacrilège*.

THE LOCKERT LIBRARY OF POETRY IN TRANSLATION